NATIONAL SERVICE



# THE EARLY LIFE OF JACK DARBY 1933-1954

**Enlisted by King George VI** **Discharged by QUEEN ELIZABETH II**

## CORONATION OF QUEEN ELIZABETH II

**by Jim Burton.**

-------------------------------------------

FOR BARRIE.

Jim Burton
2018.



**DEDICATION.**

IN MEMORY OF MY TWO BROTHERS WHO ALSO SERVED IN THE RAF.

JOHN FREDERICK BURTON RAF REGIMENT.

WILLIAM ARTHUR BURTON RAF.

WHO SERVED DURING THE SAME PERIOD.

ALSO TO ALL THOSE OTHER VETERANS WHO

MUST ALL NOW BE WELL INTO THER EIGHTIETH YEAR.

## SYNOPSIS.

***Jack*** **was born in 1933 without being over privileged or under privileged.**

**The story shows his growth to maturity, having survived the blitz he looks forward to joining his heroes as one of the elite pilots of the new jet age.**

**It is a light hearted look at life in the fabulous fifties, with his first stop gap job with it's exposure to the opposite sex.**

**The humour attached to the basic training in the RAF in 1951.**

**The background and life style of King Farouk of Egypt is examined to show the part his character plays in the story.**

**Jack and an American CIA officer, meet a Russian KGB officer in Birmingham. An American Sergeant trys to sell secrets obtained by his English girl friend to the KBG.**

**Will the characterless bird brained American Sargent gets eliminated before his promise to marry the dour RAF typist Olga can be put to the test?**

**A sub plot involves a senior aircraftswoman Thelma who is stamped with a TOP SECRET stamp; while she does not complain about this her less attractive colleague who was not stamped reports the incident, and as a result this a Corporal nearly loosed his stripes.**

**The identity of the person who reported the amorous Thelma is revealed.**

**The secret of the TOP SECRET stamp is exposed for all to see, provided they will pay for a copy of the photograph.**

**Jack finally emerges a more mature and street wise individual following his grass roots involvement in the affairs of state.**

Table of Contents

CHAPTER.

CHAPTER 1.

## MEMORIES

Jack, was born in the summer of 1933 in Sorrento not the town in sunny Italy, but a hospital in Birmingham where all difficult arrivals were dealt with, that was the year Adolph Hitler came to power in Germany.

An engine failure caused an aeroplane to land in Hyde Park, during the changing of the Guard, and it is the last year a team of horses will be used to launch a lifeboat in England.

He had always wanted to learn to fly. War, aeroplanes, and horses were to have a big influence over the course of his life.

As a young child living in Spark hill Birmingham he remembered the excitement when the men called to install electricity in the house, this meant an end to going to the shop to have the wireless battery charged. It also meant an end to lighting the gas, and broken gas mantles; those delicate creations by which a flame of dull blue gas is spread to form a delicate tracery of gentle yellow light. The gas man still came with his ladder and pole to extinguish the street light in the morning.

Jack's bed room, an unlighted attic, welcomed this kindly light. Never- the-less he was none too happy when the candle that had seen him to bed was extinguished.

Just before the outbreak of the war, we moved into a house in a pleasant suburb on the outskirts of Birmingham called Billesley Common.

What excitement there was when the delivery men called bringing bread and milk to the door. The horses seemed to know where to stop, while the men made their deliveries, or enjoyed a 'cuppa ' at selected houses. A feed bag was slung under the horses head, buckets of water were provided by enthusiastic children, all accompanied by much patting and stroking of manes and coats.

Less popular were the coal delivery men who with their black coal dusted faces and rougher manners,did not have the appeal of the more smartly dressed bread and milk rounds men.

They were also less liked, because when an adventurous boy ran and hung on the back of the cart for a free ride, he would be dislodged by an unceremonious flick of the driver's whip.

School days were nearly always a pleasure, there was always something new to see, learn, or do. Sundays meant Sunday school. I think this welcomed by our parents, because it gave them a quiet hour.

My first disappointment with the opposite sex happened at five years of age, Mary the same age as myself handed me a large block of Cadbury's chocolate over the garden fence. My previous experience of sweets had been limited to a half- penny worth, in a little triangular bag, purchased on Friday night when father was paid. My joy is short lived because when I tore the wrapper off the bar of chocolate I saw only cardboard squares of chocolate. My howls of dismay, brought mother running , who attempted to explain that these are commercial travellers samples, and that they belonged to Mary's father a representative for Cadburys at Bourneville.

These pleasant days were interrupted when Mr Chamberlain the Prime Minister announced that 'we are now at war with Germany'. Even at that young age we knew that matters were serious. The boy who sat in front of me in class, named Kurt disappeared from the classroom. We asked “Where is Kurt?" We were told by the teacher that "Kurt and his parents were being 'interned for the duration'."

We were all given gas masks, together with cardboard boxes to keep them in, and made to carry them at all times. There were posters on the wall which said “Hitler will send no warning, so always carry your gas mask." The very small children were given "Mickey Mouse” gas masks these were supposed to be less frightening. When the air raid sirens sounded we were led by the teachers in a crocodile into the Air Raid Shelters and seated on wooden benches facing each other clutching our gas masks.

We sang songs to keep cheerful, and on occasions to take our minds off the anti- aircraft gun fire and the whistling sound of bombs. At the time we did not seem so afraid of the incendiary bombs, but the high explosive bombs sent shudders down our spines. We knew that there would be no escape from a direct hit.

Gerry did not get all his own way when we came out of school one day a German plane, more or less intact had crashed on the piece of waste land opposite the main school gate. We were instructed not to go anywhere near the aircraft by the teacher's. We could not resist going to inspect the aircraft. We hoped to be able to 'snaffle' a souvenir from the plane. There were two or three soldiers guarding the wreckage.

We were told to 'hop it'. Such was our curiosity that short of them charging us with rifles and fixed bayonets nothing would satisfy us but a closer view of the aircraft.

It would be true to say, at this time, that not many people would have seen an aircraft close up, let alone an enemy aircraft.

The soldiers were good natured men, bored probably now by their own company and the empty aircraft so they humoured us by answering our questions.

"Was the pilot dead?" being our first question.

"Yes" came the reply.

"Was he a big blonde man?" was our next question.

We had all heard from our parents that the Germans were breeding a super race, although we had no idea how this would be achieved.

We did see into the cockpit of the single seated aircraft and saw stains on the seat and floor. Our ambition to obtain scraps of fabric, metal, shrapnel, or ammunition from the aircraft was stopped this time; because we gave our words of honour to the soldiers that we would not 'nick' anything; if we were allowed to see the wreckage.

We would not have under any circumstances broken our word.

We were only disappointed by the absence of a dead German from the cockpit.

On another occasion, we were amazed to see that an anti-aircraft Barrage Balloon had come down on a piece of ground, just up from the site where we had seen the aircraft. This to our eyes was an incredible sight looking to us something like an over-grown elephant. As school boys we were intrigued to be informed by our elder's that women's knickers could be made from balloon and parachute fabric, and much sniggering and speculation was indulged in.

During the 'Blitz' most families spent quite a long time in their air raid shelters. These Anderson metal shelters had to be fitted into the ground, and then the roof covered with earth to the depth of two or three feet. They were just big enough to have double bunk beds fitted each side of the entrance with a space in the middle for a small cot or table. All our neighbours had one in their garden.

We did not have one my father resolutely refusing to erect one, instead at the height of the bombing; mother; two brothers and I were crouched under the stairs while the bombs whistled down, night after night.

Father meanwhile stayed in his armchair.

The drone of the aircraft, the whistling sound as they dropped their bombs, followed by a brief moment of silence, then the thud and noise of the explosion, heralded the sense of relief at not feeling the full impact of the bombs; it meant that they had fallen some distance away, and we could breathe again, that emotion would never be forgotten.

One night a whole block of houses was destroyed, not a hundred yards from where we crouched. That night a concerned neighbour came to us and insisted that we go down into their shelter. Father still would not move.

After the raid finished we went back into the house. Father was still sitting in his chair, with most of the front room windows blown in, by the shock waves from the bombs that had demolished the houses not many yards from us.

Father's logic being that the Germans had not been able to kill him during his five years in France during the First World War, so the chances of him being killed as a non-combatant in this one were considerably less. As for us we had to take our chance.

Those windows helped by the brown sticky paper that had been applied to stop broken glass from flying about that survived the blast, were joined by a variety of cardboard squares or plywood squares until replacement glass could be obtained. Some of our windows remained in that condition for a long time.

Father resolutely maintaining that as Hitler had blown them out, Hitler could pay for them to be replaced.

Jack replaced these windows when glass became available at the end of the war in Europe in 1945.

Mother on the other hand was a kind hard working woman who did her best to cloth and feed us, makes do and mend was a way of life for everyone, with clothing and food rationed. N ew trousers for little boys were made from worn out men's trousers.

One day on the way to school while travelling on the top deck of the tram along the Alcester Road, in Kings Heath Birmingham I saw a bomb falling from an aircraft and was fascinated to see it land in the middle of the road at Alcester Lanes end. The fractured water main sent a great fountain of water skywards. From my standing position on the open end of the top deck of the tram I had a wonderful view of the action.

The aircraft turned away, then banked, and came back firing his machine guns at the tram and any other targets in his view. Fortunately I copied the example of the adults and lay on the floor of the tram and avoided being hit.

On a lighter note we played marbles along the gutter on the way home from school, there being no traffic at all on the side roads, the odd horse and cart and a few cycles excepted.

As the war progressed and the threat of invasion receded, we were invaded by a new breed of men. These were the Yanks to young boys they appeared to be very glamorous figures.

There were also some darker swarthier men with cheeky dark eyes, who wore strange uniforms with roundels on their backs. These were the Italian POW's, let out of the camp to work on the land. These strangers seemed to be the subject of admiration for the women and girls, but they were distrusted by the few men left at home.

Near the end of the hostilities I attended a ' boy's only' Grammar School. The war had the effect that retired teachers and lady teachers had to be employed while the younger men were away serving in the armed forces. One old master who was recalled whose job entailed teaching Grammar to the first year boys put this proposition to us, one morning. "What would you rather do to-day boys, Grammar, or spelling for halfpennies?" We had one or two very profitable lessons until the Head happened to be passing the door one day.

Then the old master retired once more, disappearing to be seen no more. We were also none the wiser when a popular master, who doubled as the scout troop leader, left the school at the same time as the pretty school secretary.

About this time I joined the Air Training Corps having learnt that there would be an annual camp and a chance of having an air experience flight. My friends and I arrived at RAF Valley on Anglesey. The great day came and we climbed aboard an Avro Anson aircraft, with a great roar of engines we left the ground. The pilot instructed me to turn a handle, and it was with great pride that I wound up the under carriage. Banking the aircraft the pilot took us higher and higher, over the sea, and round the Island of

Anglesey, performing a number of manoeuvres that brought up more than apprehension for some of the budding airmen. The sight of small brown and green fields about the size of postage stamps alternating with sea and sky was too much for some. Unfortunately the demands of study at school forced us to leave the ATC within a few months of joining. At least the seeds had been sown and we would have the opportunity to pursue this interest later if we wished to.

There was now a great feeling of optimism in the country and we knew that we were going to beat Hitler and that there would be a great future for us all old and young.

All the bombed houses, factories, shops, would have to be rebuilt. There would be jobs for all after the war.

For most young men there were two years to be spent before we were called up to do our National Service. There were a great number of opportunities available to us I became a junior clerk with the local Electricity Board. The office being full of interesting characters who in the main had returned from the war, It became a source of interest for me to observe how some men had kept their ranks. Despite denials, there was an understandable distinction between those who had held rank in his Majesty's armed forces Major Farrington-Smyth, Captain Caunt, and those who had been 'erks' or 'squaddies'.

My own particular mentor, who sat facing me, was called 'Sid '.

Sydney Evans had served as an air gunner during the war.

"Why did you become an air gunner?" I asked him.

"The money and the 'tapes.' Sid replied.

"The sergeants chevrons, dummy" came as the good natured answer to my next question.

Starting work in an office that employed young women opened up an extra dimension on my life. The effect that young women had on men, were certainly understood by them, but certainly not by me. My powers of comprehension in this respect at the age of sixteen were very limited.

Penny Green would come into our general office from the drawing office and lean over Sid's shoulder, giving a number of men the benefit of a sight of her not inconsiderable cleavage.

Those who were behind her as she leant forward were rewarded with the flash of black stockings and multi coloured petticoats which flared out from her fine hips.

My understandable admiration of these attractions was not missed by the eagle eyed Sid.

"You want to be careful of that one" said my mentor, but he would not be drawn on the subject.

"You went to an all boys' school didn't you" said Sid.

Much to my embarrassment I had to admit this fact to him.

"We were next door to the girls' school" I said. "There was a high brick wall separating us. They used to let us out at different times, so we could not make contact with them, against school rules to talk to them," I confessed lamely.

At last Christmas came round and this allowed me to be introduced to that great social leveller, at least for a short period, the annual office party. The drawing boards were pushed to one side, a record player introduced and desks groaning with food and even more drink was placed around the edges of the large office. We sat around talking, gossiping, and drinking glasses of different types of alcohol that I had never seen, let alone tasted before. To my great delight Penny Green who had been the subject of a lot of attention from the men in the office, came over to me and said "Care to dance?" She guided my stumbling footsteps around the floor clasping me in her arms.

After a few turns round the floor we ended up behind the tall green filing cabinets that formed a partition along one side of the office. We found that we were kissing passionately in a way I had not known before. I also discovered out that a mixture of alcohol can produce a very sweet tasting kiss. My hand was around her waist, when I felt it being lifted and placed on her breast. “There you have wanted to do that," she said with a knowing smile. "Yes" I replied and slipped my hand inside her blouse. She turned slightly encouraging my fingers to penetrate her bra, the round firmness of her breast felt red hot in the palm of my hand.

"Hello Jack, when are you coming up for air?"

“I think it time for my dance, Penny," said Sid who suddenly appeared from around the corner.

I was left leaning against the wall while the 'air gunner ' waltzed off with the girl.

I noticed that Sid's whirling her around gave the maximum effect to the display of coloured petticoats that were displayed briefly each time they turned. Penny's slim waistline being emphasised by a wide belt that separated her blouse from the skirt. They made a handsome couple on the dimly lit improvised dance floor.

I do not remember very much more about that party, except that I was guided to my bus by my guardian Sid, who evidently paid my fare and instructed the bus conductor to deposit me at the nearest bus stop to my home.

After the Christmas break Penny continued to flirt with us when her duties allowed, Sid said "That I had had a lucky escape,” and that there would be plenty of other opportunities for a young man like me.

Everybody kept telling me what a wonderful thing it is to be young, but I was racked with insecurity and envious of the self-confidence of the men in the office who had returned from the war.

There being one exception, a man called Cyril, who for no obvious reason would suddenly bang on the side of the two green filing cabinets that stood either side of his desk and yell, "Let me out! Let me out! On asking Sid why Cyril did it Sid replied with just two words

"He's barmy."

Looking back on those earlier days everything seemed that much clearer and simpler. If you committed a crime and you were caught you knew you would be punished.

People respected their elders, who it was acknowledged normally knew best. A fraternal feeling existed in most places of employment and a sense of sharing a common experience.

Simplistic it may have been, but the day when conflicting opinions on the psychology of the mind, framed in terms of almost incomprehensible legal jargon had not yet arrived to confuse us.

Growing up during the war my greatest heroes were those intrepid young men who were pilots during the battle of Britain; Douglas Bader, Peter Townsend, Johnnie Johnson, and all those airmen who had saved Britain in her hour of need. The desire to follow in their footsteps amounted almost to an obsession.

Aircraft recognition, the ability to identify enemy aircraft became an essential part of everyday living. To recognise a Junkers 87, Heinkel, or a Messerschmitt was every bit as important, if not more, than to recognise the Spitfire or Hurricane. No doubt our enthusiasm was to some extent fired by the comics that we read, The Hotspur, The Rover, and The Wizard.

My regret then at being too young to take part in the fight to defeat the Nazis, was tempered by the talk about the bullshit that had to be endured by every serviceman. There were tales of scrubbing barrack room table tops white, polishing floors until you could see your face in them, and then scraping the handles of the brooms and dry scrubbers with razor blades until they were white.

Kit inspections requiring equipment to be laid out on the bed in a specific order, and if any item was not in its correct place, or a speck of dust found resulting in shrieks of 'idle man ' or 'filth' by bullying NCO's with the bed being turned over, were I thought exaggerated, or a wind up by the ex-servicemen.

How wrong can you be?

## CHAPTER 2

## DO YOU RIDE?

After spending two years working in the offices of the Electricity Board I resolved that whatever I would do I would not spend the rest of my life crouched over an office desk.

This incredible boredom only being relieved by the occasional lunch time visit to the cinema up the road, that showed Flash Gordon films "Conqueror of the Universe" and the like. It was possible by eating one's sandwiches, while working, that time could be created to get full value from these mid - day films.

My father, Harry , an 'old contemptible' had been wounded, and gassed in the first world war, and like many of his generation had not really ever fully recovered from the horrors of trench war fare. His word was law in our house and he forbade me from joining the army.

Among his gems of wisdom was that second class riding was better that first class marching, and that I would not learn anything of any use for Civilian life in the infantry.

I did not appreciate at that time just what good advice he had given me.

Part of the master plan to keep out of the army was to volunteer to join the RAF. The war in Korea had begun to cast its shadow over a new rising generation.

In due course, I joined the Royal Air Force, the Brylcream boys as they were sneeringly referred to by members of the army. They in their turn were referred to as "brown jobs", providing when in there company we out-numbered them by at least two to one.

I accordingly went to the recruiting Office in Dale End Birmingham and enquired if they had any vacancies for trainee pilots. My enquiry was received by a sergeant, with that special look cultivated by a Senior N.C.O. for simpletons and maniacs.

I was then ushered in to the presence of an officer who displayed the coveted Flying badge on his tunic on top of a row of medal ribbons that proved him to be a pukka flying type. The results of the fairly simple tests, I had taken, were put in front of him, and my School Certificate. This qualified me to be called for further aptitude test to be conducted at RAF Hornchurch in Essex. I was told that they would give me a railway warrant and that I would be the guest of the RAF for three days. The officer was extremely pleasant and wished me well. An airman who had been sitting in the outer office appeared and showed me out of the office.

How civilised I thought.

I enquired "Do you want me for anything else, Sir?"

"You don't call me sir, if you want me you call Shag," said the airman; wearing the single bladed propeller on the side of his tunic, which indicated his rank as Leading Aircraftsman.

"No you can "F" off!"

I returned home and waited anxiously for the arrival of the railway warrant.

After a few weeks, that seemed interminably long, I received the warrant,

Changed it at the railway station, and set out for Hornchurch somewhere in Essex.

I had never been to London, now at just under eighteen years of age I was on my way.

My directions were that I would have to change trains at Euston, travel on the underground, and then catch another train to Hornchurch.

I duly arrived in London and having some time to spare before catching my mainline train to Hornchurch I decided to explore London. After seeing the House of Commons and Buckingham Palace, I decided to walk through Green Park, where I was approached by this attractive young lady.

The lady asked me, "Have you got the time?"

I looked at my naked wrist and said with complete innocence,

"I am sorry but I don't have a watch."

She gave me what can only be described as a pitying smile and passed on her way.

I duly arrived at Hornchurch Station where I was pleasantly surprised to see a dozen or so young men who were on the same hop waiting for transport to RAF Hornchurch. We were transported to a reception area and allocated places in a Nissan hut that was set aside for aircrew hopefuls.

At the mess hall we ate our first meal which was superior to many that followed. Food still being rationed, we were all well pleased at the quantity we were given.

The next day we were put in the care of aircrew assessors who were in the main Corporals. The first part of the selection procedure consisted of a full day of medical tests. They tested everything. One vivid memory for me while jumping up and down off a chair and having my pulse taken at intervals; was of hearing a woman screaming or laughing in the next room, and then being asked. "What would my reaction be if she came into the room naked?"

I replied that" It would at least raise my pulse rate".

This seemed to amuse the examiner.

At night in the billet we swopped yarns as we lay in our beds. We were mainly eighteen year olds, but there were one or two older men about twenty one years of age or so, who had either been to university or finished some training course that had delayed their admission to the services. William Stephens, one of these older more experienced men, who had served in the Royal Navy, prior to attending this selection centre, regaled us with a story about the treatment for venereal disease. This according to the 'old sweat' consisted of having an instrument inserted into the opening of the penis, the instrument being shaped like a miniature umbrella. Having been inserted closed; it was then pulled out, opening up as it was withdrawn. The resulting action was to scrape the inside of the organ clean with the little blades that revolved round the frame of the instrument. The accuracy of his statements was not challenged, and a billet of impressionable young men went to sleep, determined to avoid the venal perils.

The next morning we were engaged in various tasks; one of them consisted of fixing a variety of wooden pegs of different shapes and sizes into holes that did not appear at first sight capable of accepting them. However it was all good fun.

This activity being broken up by sitting various written papers designed to reveal our basic understanding of the theory of flight, in respect of heavier than air aircraft; also our understanding of things mechanical.

Our abilities to think logically under conditions of stress and to react quickly in emergency situations were thoroughly tested.

One of the more interesting tests involved sitting in a type of basic link trainer. This consisted of a cockpit complete with elementary flying controls, so that the potential trainee pilot would be able to get the feel of an aircraft while still on the ground, with no danger either to himself or to anyone else. The basic rudder control consisted of pressing the right rudder bar with my right foot, this made the nose of the aircraft move to the right, by pressing the left rudder with my left foot, and this made the nose of the aircraft move to the left. At the same time by holding the control column with my hand, and moving the control column to the right the aircraft banked to the right, or by moving the control column to the left the aircraft banked to the left. A slight back pressure on the stick and I climbed, or a slight forward pressure and I descended.

The instruments in front of me indicate my position in relation to the ground. In order to make things more difficult, there is a battery of different coloured warning lights that keep coming on and going off. The intention is to switch off the red lights as they come on, while ignoring the others, and at the same time trying to fly the simulator. The aim being to retain control, remain in the air, and not crash on to the ground.

Many trainees found to their great surprise that they had either crashed, or had spent most of their time trying to fly several hundred feet under the ground!

The selection procedure was very thorough, strict and fair, for what we realised even at this stage was a very demanding profession.

The final day and interview arrived and we were escorted individually into a room at the end of which was a table. Behind the table sat an impressive body of men, some of them to our eyes quite old, one of them I thought would have been well over thirty years of age!

On the table in front of them lay a row of caps, some with gold braid on the peaks. Most of them wore the full flying badge of a pilot, or the half wing worn by navigators, air engineers, and air gunners, on their tunics. One of the interviewers, however, did not display the coveted flying badge on his tunic.

The usual questions were asked "Why do you want to fly?"

"Have you had any flying experience?"

"We are gradually replacing piston engine aircraft by the new Gloster Meteor jet fighter."

"Do you know that after basic training most pilots will be trained on jets?”

"Do you know that we only accept a very small percentage of applicants for flying duties? “

These questions were asked and the answers given to the best of my ability.

The next question which came from the ground crew officer was

"Do you wide?"

At least that is how the question sounded like to me.

I replied that," I rode a B.S.A. Bantam motor Cycle."

"Horses boy!” “Horses boy!" was the somewhat testy retort.

I replied that I did not ride horses, but thought it prudent not to mention the fact that the only horses I had come in contact with were those drawing the Co-Op bread van, or the coal cart. I have, long since, reflected, many times, on the inability of some of the upper classes to pronounce their "r's ". The logic of the question escaped me at the time, and its relevance to flying still escapes me to this day. Had the selection procedure been aimed to recruit potential officers for an exclusive Cavalry regiment, it might have just made sense.

During the war, which had only finished a matter of five or six years ago there had been published "The Defence ABC painting book" for children. Like many children I had painted the pictures and taken in the messages.

"A" was "for Airmen already to fly."

"L" was for "Lancers where men of all ranks, had given up horses and taken to tanks."

I wondered if that particular gentleman had assimilated those messages.

The interviews were concluded and we were told that we would be informed in due course if our applications were successful.

I the event I was informed several weeks later that I had not been successful due to my lack of mechanical knowledge.

Stuff them I thought ----- just because I can't ride a bloody horse.

## CHAPTER 3.

## RAF RECRUIT TRAINING.

The day arrived when with the encouragement of Sid I went to the RAF recruiting Office for the second time to volunteer to become one of his Majesty's airmen.

A few weeks later I reported to RAF Cardington to be kitted out. This famous airfield once housed the R101 Airship that crashed in France, with considerable loss of life a generation ago, and virtually finished the military use of airships. It is a moving experience to see the plaque commemorating this event.

It was moving in a different sense when we were paraded in the old airship hanger, to be bellowed at from store to store, to pick up every item of kit that we would require. These two old hangers were like caverns, with important exception that they were above ground. In one corner of the hanger a group a men were being encouraged to jump into space connected to a parachute harness. The eaves of the hanger were so high that the men waiting to be dispatched seemed to be like Lilliputians. On reaching the ground they were running back to the scaffolding to climb back up for the next jump.

This we did not envy, we were too busy with our own tasks to spare but a passing thought for them.

Having collected our kit we then bundled all our civilian clothing into brown paper parcels, and surrendered then to the authorities, who assured us they would be despatched to our homes.

Resplendent in our blue battle dress, kit bags over our shoulders we then went off to receive our basic training.

We were told that it would be at least two months before we would be fit to be seen in public. So we were driven away in closed troopers to do our square bashing. This was calculated to turn us from sloppy teen-agers into fighting men. Having been formed into training flights and squadrons we began training for real.

Before this event however there was the ritual that was looked forward to with relish by the training NCO's, but with great apprehension by the more trendy of the intake this being the obligatory haircut, that was inflicted on every recruit, whether he needed one or not. There were one or two recruits who sported the DA haircut, politely known as the 'ducks tail', the initials obviously standing for another more basic aspect of the ducks anatomy. The camp 'barbers' took a sadistic delight in cutting the locks of the trendier individuals who were reduced to the very short back and sides that was common to all servicemen.

The weeks passed very quickly, and not too unpleasantly, after you accepted that to the NCO's we were all horrible little men, and none of us had fathers.

"If you broke your mother’s heart, you won’t break mine, get fell in you horrible shower” was the more moderate type of endearment that was offered up as we were marched off at the double, to our various activities.

One recruit a solid red faced Cornish man, who had been a grave-digger before he joined up, was particularly slow in grasping instructions. He had great trouble in co-ordinating his arms and legs, partly due, to his desire to get everything right, and consequently getting into even greater trouble. The sight of him swinging his left arm forward at the same time as his left foot had to be seen to be believed, this action being quite the opposite of to the natural rhythm of marching.

When marching off with the left foot forward, the left arm swings back quite naturally for most individuals, Frank Tomb could not get it right. One morning the drill sergeant screeching at the drill corporal for an explanation for this great travesty of military discipline had the recruit out in front of the squad.

With a corporal each side of him he proceeded to march him up and down the square in front of us. The corporals had a firm hold of his arms on either side, and proceeded to work his arms up and down for him, in the required manner. After a few times the corporals were instructed to let go his arms and the drill sergeant, who always carried a large pace stick, with a silver knob on the end, stood by his side.

"We will now march correctly," he stated "if you do not, I will cut your bloody arms off." As they marched off in front of us, the pace stick was held in front of the recruits arm, and then removed and replaced in time with each step.

The recruit marched in perfect time.

As Frank Tomb said later he kept thinking "I daren't risk hitting his silver knob."

During weapon training he excelled even the drill episode. We were told that when the whistle blew we were to throw our rifles forward and fall to the ground. The rifles had a small bayonet attached to the front called a pig sticker. When the whistle blew we threw ourselves down onto the ground throwing our rifles forward, so that we then came up to the prone firing position, we had the butt of the rifle in a nice comfortable position under the chin.

Not Frank Tomb when the whistle blew, in his eagerness to please he threw his rifle and bayonet forward letting it go, and nearly impaling one of the of men in front of us. He did however finish his basic training and passed out with the rest of us. While on the subject of passing out we were paraded one day and the same Sergeant announced.

"We are giving blood to-day. This is a voluntary act.

One pace forward any man who does not wish to donate a pint. "

We were all marched off and dutifully gave our blood for our country.

A few weeks later we were all marched to the sick quarters and formed into one long line, told to look to the front. On arriving at the front of the queue we were injected in both arms simultaneously, with what we were never quite sure. Great lumps came up under our arms and we all were feeling like death, with headaches and weakness in the legs. To assist us to forget our misery we were all put to work giving the floors of the huts an extra polishing with the 'bumpers' that were so thoughtfully provided.

We were kept busy from reveille in the early morning to lights out at night.

From the time of the raucous call of 'Hands off your cocks', pull up your socks ," or similar utterance from the duty Corporal; to lights out, our time was fully taken up; with cleaning of kit and polishing of boots to fill in any spare time.

During this period some thought was given to the concern that no one had any sexual urges; and were they giving us some dreadful drug that would spoil us for the rest of our lives?

The humanity of the drill Corporal was confirmed when he told us 'they' put bromide into the mess tea, to control us lesser mortals during basic training, but to our relief this was not the practice at normal RAF stations. We had suspected something, because the mess tea tasted very different from the NAAFI tea which we purchased during our breaks.

They also kept their promise, although we did not believe them at the time, that by the end of our training we would be the fittest that we would ever be in our lives At long last we were granted a 48 hour pass, and allowed to go home for the weekend. We had to be back by 23.59 hours on the Sunday night.

My train was running late and I arrived back seven minutes late. Six minutes after midnight. On a charge for being AWOL (absent without leave), I was marched in front of the squadron commander.

"Accused and escort, left right, left right, halt".

I was asked “how did I plead?”

I thought it best to plead guilty.

The charge was read, the sergeant gave his evidence, and after all he had been on the same train as me from his weekend leave.

"Three days confined to camp, fined one day's pay”.

“Do you accept my punishment, or do you elect to be tried by Court Martial?"

By now I was quite thankful to accept this punishment.

One of the joys of the training NCO's was to bellow at the trainees for any minor transgressions "Your feet won't touch the ground, you horrible, horrible, horrible little man."

This was for a time a source of silent amusement for me, who could not imagine how this feat of levitation could be performed.

I was to learn.

One Monday morning the whole of the squadron were paraded to witness the drumming out of two corporals who had been sentenced to be dismissed the service. Four gigantic service policemen had the unfortunate individuals handcuffed to them. The policemen were on each side of the prisoner's.

A Senior NCO bellowed for them to be doubled marched on to the square. It may have been the difference in height that accounted for part of the spectacle, but as they passed us I swear the prisoner’s feet did not touch the ground.

The dismissal grounds were read out and words to the effect that they were not fit to wear the Kings uniform. The chevrons were removed from the arms of the disgraced men. It was not a pleasant sight for any of us to witness. The prisoners were then run off the square in the same manner. The two men were homosexuals who had been heard boasting about their friendship with a peer of the realm, who had been of the same sexual persuasion.

Their biggest sin was of course being found out. Provided homosexuals kept themselves to themselves and did not interfere with the straight men they were tolerated, albeit they were the source of some ribald amusement.

The rule of thumb being that you kept clear of Nancy boys, and avoided girls with sores or spots on their mouths.

The films of soldiers suffering from venereal disease were so horrific that it is not surprising that many young servicemen accepted the advice of the medical officers that their best friend was Mrs Palmer.

The day arrived that we passed out from our recruit training; having survived the basic training that was calculated to make us into competent infantry capable of defending an airfield. We were quite proud of the fact that we could shoot a rifle reasonably well, and charge at swinging dummies with a bayonet while yelling obscenities of our own choosing. We also became part of a platoon that was able to strip down, carry then re-assemble a Bren gun and get it firing with reasonable speed and accuracy.

I was pleased to be one of the favoured ones allowed to fire a short burst from the Boffor's gun at an imaginary enemy aircraft. This I thought is far better than my earlier experience as a schoolboy on a tram being attacked by a real enemy aircraft.

They had a last go at trying to finishing us off by making us go in to a gas chamber, and on the word of command removing our gas masks, in order that we would recognise the effect of gas.

The result being stinging eyes, a nauseous feeling, and we were unable to breath properly. I thought of my father and his mates in the trenches during the First World War. The war to end all wars!

We then took part in a passing out parade, said our good -byes, and were then posted to different camps for trade training according to our various abilities.

## CHAPTER 4.
### ADMINISTRATIVE DUTIES

Having been disappointed at not being accepted for flying duties my next posting resulted in me re-mustering to train to become part of that section of the RAF known as the Accounting and Secretarial Branch.

Once the training was completed I became a personal clerk in an orderly room, at an RAF transit camp that received all those who had failed at some period of their training, either as aircrew or some ground trade. The airmen were put into 'pool flight ' and kept occupied by doing any jobs about the camp until they were re-mustered into another trade.

Keith Smart and I were detailed one day to take a party of airmen to the ‘Section’ that handed out the tools for gardening. Gardening was a loose term for any activity that involved the issue of spades, forks and hoe's. In charge of the store was a Warrant officer general duties, the back bone of the discipline of the other ranks. In his case he held his position by virtue of long service rather than any other qualification.

The drill was that you were handed or took a tool and then you signed for it. One smart young man, a failed aircrew trainee, noticeable because of the absence of the eagle shoulder flashes or shite hawks as they were colloquially known, took a hoe.

“Excuse me Sir, he said.   "How do you spell hoe?"

“What lad dont you know how to spell hoe! Put it back! And 'tek' a shovel."

You just did not get one over the old time W.O.'s.

Keith Smart and I became friends when we both signed on for a three years regular engagement.  Keith is about the same height and builds as myself standing six feet tall, with a medium to large frame, his most distinguishing feature being his shock of red hair.

Keith completed his basic training with me and at twenty one years of age had completed a degree course at university before coming into the RAF, and he intended to become a chartered accountant on completing his service.  Shortly after the gardening job, someone must have looked at his academic record and decided that he might be suitable to be commissioned in the secretarial branch of the service.  Keith disappeared and then reappeared three days later to tell me that the interviews went well as far as the paper qualifications went, but they had decided that he would be better left in his present position , unless he was prepared to sign on for twelve years after completing the necessary officer training.

Keith was a Yorkshire man and to be perfectly honest, he had a terrific accent.  He was not the easiest of men to understand, especially when he got excited.  One of the questions put to him was

"Where do you come from?"

The proud reply was "Uddersfield"

This had produced a mixed reception from the examining board.  Keith reckoned that they did not like his accent, and it was beyond his comprehension that any person could think his speech odd.

"It's you buggers that speak queer" was his retort to any ragging from anyone who did not come from Yorkshire in general or Huddersfield in particular.

The RAF in their wisdom then decided to post me to the Administrative Office that was responsible for staff that worked at the giant Record Office. This proved to be a cushy number, because although we lived on the camp we travelled by trooper to the Record Office each day. By the nature of the work there were many WRAF and civilians employed in the huge administrative buildings. All postings to anywhere in the world were controlled from here, and the personal details of every serving airman were carefully recorded. What an opportunity for any dissident to throw a spanner in the works. The administrative office was manned by a Warrant officer, a Corporal, two Airmen, and two members of the women's Royal Air Force.

Next door and opening into this office, was the office of the Flight Lieutenant who acted as adjutant to the Wing Commander.

The Wing Commander an accountant, not an ex-flyer was regarded with respect but not with quite the same admiration as some of the more junior officers who wore the flying badge.

After a short period the Corporal achieved promotion to sergeant and was posted away, I received promotion to Corporal to fill his place. The reason for my promotion was something to do with the fact that I 'understood' the Wing Commanders establishment charts. These had to be kept up to date, to show by trade and rank every person on the camp. These figures in their turn were the basis for the allocation of money, rations and resources, the larger the number of people on the establishment the more promotions for officers and men.

We had to take our turn in mounting guard at night in the main camp, and also a night patrol in the buildings in which we were working. This being due to the fact that the records staff worked a night shift because of the conflict in Korea, and other commitments to provide people for special duties.

One night while acting as deputy guard commander at the main camp we had some excitement that we could well have managed without. The Guard when they were not patrolling around the camp slept in a hut opposite the main guardroom. The guardroom being staffed by the RAF police it also contained the cells .The occupants of the cells had to be visited at intervals by the duty officer accompanied by the NCO in charge of the guard, to see if all was well.

We entered the guardroom under the eyes of the reproachful or should I say the stern eyes of the policemen who seemed to regard us as trespassers in their Kingdom. 'Abandon hope all ye who enter in' seemed to be the spirit generated by these custodians of the military law. We went down the corridor to the cells, the cell door was flung open and we looked inside.

Hanging from the cell window bars appeared to be the body of an airman.

The rope attached to the window bar held the head at an awkward angle, the beret on the head was not worn at the regulation angle, the body from the neck downwards being clothed in fatigue overalls, and the boots were hanging from the bottom of the trousers.

"O my God what's happened?" yelled the young officer, turning very white.

Suddenly from behind the cell door there jumps an apparition dressed only in a pair of RAF issue white underpants. “I am going for a run “ he said. The man ran past the police men, out of the guard room, and out of the camp pursued by the policemen.

We examined the body, and the officer now recovered from the shock pronounced that it was very ingenious the way it had been constructed. The overalls had been filled by the airman with all his normal uniform clothing, and the head had been made out of socks and under-wear.

"I suppose we had better send some of our lads after him" said Pilot Officer Ray, quietly enjoying the discomfort of the police.

"Perhaps we should give them the chance to do their own dirty work Sir before we help them. They will not thank us if we catch him." I suggested.

"Good thinking Corporal we will make the sods sweat" Replied the National Service officer.

We were saved the trouble anyway because within ten minutes the prisoner was recaptured and placed in his cell by the furious policemen.

We understood later that he was confined in his cell in just his underpants for the night. That undoubtedly cooled his ardour.

The police took charge of the dummy for evidence. The next day the airman appeared before the Commanding Officer charged with trying to escape from lawful custody. I never found out what happened to him, because he was sent to a psychiatric hospital for tests. The camp grape vine said he was trying to work his ticket, because he was due for a posting to the Far East.

After the end of World War 2, Korea was temporarily occupied by the Soviet Union in the north and the USA in the south, negotiations to reunify the country failed. Elections to decide the political future were only held in the south. After these the new South Korean Government declared its independence.

The communists invaded the south in 1950.

We had sent our forces to repel the communists, among them the "Glorious Gloucester's whose home base Robins Wood Camp was just up the road in a manner of speaking from our camp. The Glosters had fought with great courage at the Imjin River during April of 1951. Many families in the town had received letters from the War Office stating their sons had been reported 'Missing', 'Killed in Action' or Missing believed to be a 'POW'. The men who had returned wounded from this confrontation were only too willing to spread rumours of the kind; they are going to send all you lot all to Korea.

We were not over enthusiastic to be sent to fight the Chinese who we were told were armed mainly with light machine guns.

Our main weapon being the single shot bolt action 303 Lee Enfield rifle with a magazine that contained ten rounds.

The conflict dragged on for over three years and by the time a truce was called about two million people died. We all knew that the Korean troops were fanatical in their loyalty to their leader Kim Ll-sung. He was known as the 'Great Leader', 'His Excellency', or perhaps more modestly as 'the greatest Genius Mankind has Ever Known'.

With Chinese 'volunteers' sent by Mao Zedong to aid their brothers, Korea was not the posting that was desired by those who wanted a quiet life and to live long enough to enjoy it.

Many airmen considered that protecting the fuel dumps, from the thieving airmen in the next billet, who were pilfering coke to heat their own quarters was enough excitement for them.

Our routine was pleasantly disturbed when the Mayor of Cheltenham decided to host a dance to promote Anglo American Friendship. There being a large American airbase situated not far from our camp. We were to be treated to a free dance and reception at the town hall. What a wonderful thought.

A social occasion presented an opportunity for the RAF to mix with the American Air force in order to cement friendship between the two allies who proudly wore blue uniforms. We arrived at the town hall all dressed up in our best blue uniforms, with our brass buttons shining, and our cap badges gleaming.

His worship the Mayor, resplendent with his chain of office over his shoulders, met us in the entrance hall, and shook hands with every man as we entered the magnificent ballroom. Standing by him were the distinguished guests, the Group Captain and his lady, and the impressive figure of the American Base Commander and his lady. Standing discreetly some distance away were the "Snow Drops" as the RAF Police was referred to; when they were not within hearing distance. The distinctive white covers worn on top of their 'cheese cutter' peaked caps served to distinguish them from the other airmen.

A little less discreetly the American Base police were distinguished by wearing very shiny white helmets, while hanging from their belts were the biggest white batons we had ever seen.

Once we entered the ballroom, at first everything was very decorous, although the RAF men tended to stick together at one end of the bar, while the bar at the other end of the room seemed to be dominated by American servicemen. Then there was another element in this equation -------women. There were WRAF girls in uniform and there were civilian girls all dressed up in their best party finery. There are probably about two servicemen to each girl; and an equal number of British servicemen and American servicemen. The evening is passing very pleasantly talking and drinking when to my amazement a resplendent be medalled figure in an American uniform came across the room to me and said

“Hello Jack how are you?"

"Well if it's not Gerald Beaufoy, it is very nice to see you" I replied.

He stood there in front of me wearing a uniform made of a smarter lighter material than mine, indeed the kind of material that our officers uniforms are made of, he looked very smart indeed.

We were the same age we used to sit behind each other at school, and we got on well together.

"What are you doing in the American Air force?"

"My mother is English but my father is American, so I had the choice of joining either of the services.  The pay is better in the American Air force."

Their pay in fact is more than double that of the British servicemen.

We could see that their uniforms were smart, although they seemed to be more casual in their dress.

"You could have joined the American Air force "said my school pal." On finishing your engagement you would have had the right to settle in the USA, if you wished."

Now he tells me I thought.

"How long have you been in the Air force Gerald?" I asked him."

"Nearly three months."

"How on earth have you been able to earn two medals in such a short time?"

"One for completing my basic training, the other for serving overseas."  He replied.

I thought this a bit ripe Gerald admitted he had been born in England and then gone to Germany to do his basic training, after this they posted him back to within fifty miles of his home, here in England.

We were certainly the poor relations   when comparing the uniforms and the money we had in our pockets. We exchanged our service details and our home addresses and promised we would get in touch with each other in a few weeks' time.  The bars were doing a roaring trade and with the occasional taunt, and exchange of obscenities between the rival air forces everything was going with a swing.

The real problem developed around the dance floor where the RAF boys were in the main losing the battle to obtain partners for the dancing. It appeared to us that all the Americans were 'shooting a line' to impress the ladies.

With-out exception they gave the impression that they were millionaires, or at least owned ranches in Texas, or apartments in New York, when asking for the pleasure of their company for a dance, the extreme courtesy they extended to the ladies could not be matched by many of our own home grown Romeo's.

From the first time they spoke they invariable addressed them as ma'am, in what must have been intriguing and irresistible accents. In general terms the American servicemen were hated, despised, and envied in turn, by their contemporaries in the British forces.

The real trouble started when a number of RAF men attempted to "Excuse me", during the dancing. They also did not know, or chose to ignore, the custom that a man was able by taping the dancer on the shoulder, take his place on the dance floor for the remainder of that dance. The Americans were not going to give up their partners just when they thought they were making some progress.

We did not take kindly to their loudly expressed opinions regarding the availability of a 'nice bit of ass'. I heard the response "Push off Mack" in a broad transatlantic accent, to several requests to give up partners in an excuse me quick step.

Suddenly there was scuffle women shrieked the atmosphere changed dramatically from bawdy good natured banter to an atmosphere charged like a thunderstorm, with the warm scent of compliant women being rapidly replaced by the smell of sweating cursing men.

Tables were overturned and glasses and bottles thrown and suddenly the ballroom was transformed into a battlefield. Everywhere sides are being taken and gangs of RAF men are fighting bands of Yanks. The fighting became very vicious, and the wearing of one uniform or another is sufficient justification to take a swing at any one not wearing the same uniform.

Suddenly there is a loud blowing of whistles and the police ordered everyone out of the room. This is ignored by the more dedicated fighters on both sides.

I made my way out of the room as the American Police charged into the melee their batons flying, the massive batons were hitting arms and legs and also many hard hits across the backs of those who were slow to move. I am glad they exercised discrimination in breaking up of the riot; ----- they only hit their own men.

The blood and sweat produced a heady atmosphere which resulted in a sense of exhilaration in some of the men. There were those who preferred a good punch up to feminine company.

The majority of the RAF who had been fighting stopped the moment the RAF police arrived.

The main cause of the fighting had now how-ever, taken their handbags and gently stolen away.

I must admit that I felt that the Mayor of Cheltenham had not been very well rewarded, for his initiative in arranging this function, designed to promote Anglo-American friendship.

The next day we were all paraded, and told that we would all be confined to camp for the weekend. This collective punishment was accepted with reasonable good grace; partly because no one had any money to go out with, and we enjoyed the fact that several Americans were reported to be in hospital as a result of their running in with our boys. I received a bit of stick about my American friend, and thought of the lost opportunity of guaranteed entry to the USA. We had been told in the very straight forward manner by our 'cousins ' last night how they had won the war in Europe for us with their technical know how. That their dollars had paid for the development of the first atomic bomb and how they had brought the war to an end in the Far East by dropping the first atomic bombs on Hiroshima and Nagasaki forcing the Japanese to surrender. This being the first time in recorded history that the Japanese homeland had been occupied by foreign troops.

By whom? The GI's of course.

All of us had seen films such as “The Battle for Burma" where it appeared that "Errol Flynn" had also won that war single handed. This type of inaccurate Hollywood heroism was deeply resented by many who had relatives and friends who had fought and suffered terribly at the hands of Japanese.

The generosity of the American government to their servicemen and the standard of their accommodation was a source of amazement to all of us who experienced it.

Sometime after the Anglo-American Friendship dance Corporal Keith Smart and I were detailed to take Flt Lt. Whitehead to the American base to record the transfer of some equipment. On arrival at the entrance to the base we were greeted quite informally by a young American officer.

We had been told that we must salute all commissioned officers irrespective of nationality or service. My pal and I swung up our smartest salutes. The regulation salutes as practised for hours on the parade ground, arm out stretched and longest way up shortest way down. The

Yank returned the compliment with a casual wave that involved touching the peak of his cap.

"Ah thank you boys." This visit proves to be a culture shock.

Instead of marching or walking around the base the Americans all seemed to be whizzing around in Jeeps and trucks. We completed our business and were invited to go their mess for a meal.

This proved to be the next big shock. In the British Armed Forces, Officer's, Non-commissioned officers, and other ranks, all eat in separate establishments. These separate dining rooms are light years apart in their furnishing, and in the way the food is presented. We were all taken in to the same great dining hall, one officer and two corporals. The two officers, our host and our own officer Flt Lieutenant Whitehead, went to collect their meal and to sit with some other officers.

Meanwhile my pal Keith and I went to the Server.

A great big cook looked at us and said “What do you want boy's,"

"What can we have was our reply?"

There was no element of choice in our cook-house you either had what was going or you had nothing

"Wanna Steak?"

"Yes please. “A funny look from the cook.

"Wanna egg on it?"

“Yes please" Another funny look from the cook

“How Many?"

"Can we have more than one?” A look almost of unbelief spreads across the face of the cook

"Look at that notice Mack"

Above the Server was a large notice in capital letters

TAKE ALL YOU WANT

BUT EAT ALL YOU TAKE

The size of the steak was equivalent to the average meat ration for a British family for a week, so we gratefully accepted two eggs 'sunny side up'. A huge piece of apple pie and ice cream followed, it was a feast.

The penalty for not eating all you took we were told was fatigues, their equivalent of our janker's. This involved doing the dirtiest and most unpleasant jobs, like cleaning out the ablutions or any cleaning job that needed doing around the camp.

Flight Lieutenant Whitehead who accompanied us was a podgy, unimpressive looking individual who wore the long service medal ribbon and the general service medal ribbon on his otherwise bare breast.

He was a very decent sort of man, but always had that rather anxious look, rather like an assistant bank manager, when the manager is about. In the Wing Commanders presence he would run about like a scalded cat.

Wing Commander Hamilton Baines, a large man with a strong face containing commanding eyes wore the general service medal ribbon on his tunic, but otherwise his chest was innocent of any kind of decoration. The Wing Commander was a very highly qualified accountant; we had been informed by his deferential adjutant.

One certain fact all the officers and airmen were in awe of him and no one crossed the 'Winco'.

With the set up at the Record Office during office hours the atmosphere between the ranks was rather less militaristic and because of the confidential and secret nature of the information we processed there was a quite relaxed atmosphere. Flight Lieutenant Whitehead had spent quite some time talking to me, and he was well aware of my disappointment at not being mustered as aircrew. My disappointment being not so great now, because during the course of our duties we received the almost daily reports of injuries and fatalities among the trainee pilots who were converting on to the Meteor Jet aircraft.

The Adjutant however did keep a file on those airmen who were considered to be suitable to be commissioned in the Administrative branch and I was pleased to be informed by him that I was on his list. With this privileged information came the pearl of wisdom that no one could make any money in the RAF until they were promoted to Squadron Leader the first senior rank for officers.

At this time many promotions went to General Duties Officers who had finished their flying careers, they then spent further years building up their pensions and gratuities at the expense of the devoted dministrative officers who had slaved for years to keep the RAF from falling apart, this being a valid a point of view from where he stood.

In charge of one of the sections, ex-aircrew Flight Lieutenant Brian Dashwood due to leave the service in a few months' time, made no secret of his contempt for high ranking 'earth worms'. However as a man who had survived flying duties during the war he was respected as a character and very popular with those whom he commanded.

Dashwood would address airmen and airwomen by their Christian names; this would be definitely classified as undue familiarity and against Queens Regulations and Air Force Discipline by the establishment.

The Wing Commander being the senior officer had a habit of sending for his junior commanders to report to his office if he wanted any information. This morning instead of reporting to the office in person, Flt. Lt. Dashwood that had a heavy night the night before sent his Flt. Sgt with the information.

This was not acceptable to the 'Winco'.

"My compliments to Mr Dashwood, tell him to report to me immediately Flt Sergeant."

"Yes, Sir" said the Flt Sgt, who himself being ex aircrew had three rows of medal ribbons on his chest below the half wing worn by a navigator. Off goes the Flt Sgt, while we wait with baited breath in the outer office.

Flt Lt. Dashwood does not appear.

The Adjutant is meanwhile making phone calls to the absent officer and evidently getting nowhere fast.

After about ten minutes the adjutant goes dashing off down the corridor to see the missing officer in his section. He returns looking even more flustered and agitated than usual. As he passes us he wipes his forehead and mutters something like "I do not know, I do not know" and disappears into the inner sanctum of the Wing Commanders Office.

After a few minutes the 'Winco' comes into our office with a face like thunder and just as he appears the ex-aircrew Flt Sgt re-appears. The Flight Sgt is a ruddy faced man, always cheerful, and smiling.

"Well Flight" snapped the Wing Commander.

"Flight Lieutenants Dashwoods compliments Sir and you are to get stuffed!"

Replied the intrepid Flight Sgt

The Winco's face is a picture of fury as he turns on his heel and marches back into his office.

The Flight Lieutenant Admin following close behind nearly fainted, and we lesser mortals could not believe our ears, kept our heads down and our mouths shut.

After a while the Adjutant could be heard lamely saying to the Flt Sgt "Why did you have to say that? Surely you could have exercised some discretion."

While the Flt Sgt with tones of injured innocence protested that he was only carrying out the orders of his superior officer, acting as a messenger.

We found out later that Flight Lieutenant Dashwood the offending officer apologised, and because of his good war record got away with doing a few extra orderly officer duties. He did not however revise his opinion of those 'desk bound bastards', and was demobbed in a few weeks' time.

Flight Lieutenant Dashwood replacement a small Squadron Leader accountant flew round the camp on a pedal cycle that was fitted with a magic wheel. This consisted of a small petrol engine about 50cc capacity attached to the rear wheel of his cycle. These machines had only just come on the market and the proud owners always drove off in a cloud of smoke, accompanied by a loud phut phut phut from the tiny engine.

The skills needed to run the modern RAF were changing

## Chapter 5.

## SOME AIRWOMEN ARE ATTRACTIVE SOME HAVE ATTITUDE.

There are two airwomen employed in the Admin Office, which also served as a Disciplinary office. One is called Olga, a small runt of a woman, who when she expresses an opinion, which isn't very often, would bewail the oppression of the ordinary people of the country by the bloated capitalists.

My pal Keith described her as ugly as a bag of spanners, with the personality of a rasp. The considered opinion of the male and female members of the office was that Olga suffered from an in-growing virginity.

This condition on camp where young single male's outnumbered females by at least fifty to one is a very rare one.

Olga however is a very accurate typist.

The other airwoman is the exact opposite she is called Thelma, she chatters incessantly and has theatrical ambitions. Thelma is a shapely girl who always manages to look as if she has just been poured into her skirt, and it is a source of great interest every time she gets up from her desk to walk any distance. She is long legged and seductive. It is a compliment to the service stitching that she does not split her uniform skirt every time she moves.

The service shirt and tie cannot disguise the generous portions that seemed to be fighting to get out every time she moves. This hazardous equipment is crowned by a bold cheerful face, in which are set a pair of dark 'come to bed eyes'. Her love life is discussed openly by her and her numerous escorts are assured of her ardour and affection. A taller more graceful woman and by her presence in the office was able to exude a dominance which Olga resented.

It was agreed by all the airmen who passed through the door of the Admin. Office that they would rather have seen Thelma scantily clad than Olga wearing her 'best blue uniform'.

Thelma however cannot type accurately.

Working as a clerk /typist Olga considered herself maltreated and unappreciated especially when Thelma was promoted to Senior Aircraftswoman a promotion that she thought should have been hers.

Olga accused Thelma of earning her promotion 'on her back'.

While it could not be denied that Thelma was popular with men in the section, Thelma also got on with most of her own sex. Olga on the other hand had a chip on her shoulder and only did that which she had to do. Olga also had not passed the trade test, which would have made her eligible for promotion from her present rank of leading aircraftswoman to Senior Aircraftswoman.

The RAF had been her only life since she had left school, so rather like a spoilt child denied sweets, by its parents, Olga decided to bide her time and punish the RAF and Thelma for what she perceived as an injustice.

Security and confidentiality are the hall-marks of our work at the Record Office. We had endured many lectures on this aspect of our work. The defection of the two diplomat traitors Guy Burgess and Donald Maclean, and then the defection of a senior British intelligence officer Harold Philby set off waves that even stretched to our rural backwater in Gloucestershire in 1954.

Donald Maclean and his charming wife Melinda had lived in Cairo while he had been counsellor at the British Embassy. They were a good looking couple and had many friends among the smart people. The smart British facade hid the Moscow-orientated agent well. Maclean's lack of caution and his indiscretions would not appear to make him a good candidate to engage in espionage. It was this indiscretion and wild behaviour that led to him being thrown out of Egypt. The British Embassy had to send him out of Egypt after he wrecked the flat of an American girl in the smart suburb of Zamalek ..

## Chapter 6

## King Farouk.

King Faud of Egypt divided his time between three royal residences, the palaces of Abdin, Koubbeh and Montazah.

Abdin palace was the official residence and was somewhat similar to Buckingham Palace, Koubeh Palace was set in vast gardens in a suburb of Cairo and housed King Faud's harem.

The third royal palace was that of Montazah in Alexandria. It was in this beautiful home overlooking the sea that a young man who was destined to become the last King of Egypt spent his formative summers with his four pretty sisters.

They were firmly ruled by Mrs Naylor the British governess, who would not allow any quarrelling or augment. The children lacked for nothing, living in luxury, surrounded by adoring servants and aunts. They were over protected and naïve, one of the main entertainment' being the showing of Shirley Temple films. Whenever any enquired as to suitable presents it was always British books.

These ranged from J.M. Barry's Water Babies to Captain John's Biggles.

Young Farouk and his sisters had no contact with the real world. Outwitting the Governess became a major interest for the boy, by promises and bribes he was able to get members of the palace staff to obtain forbidden items, such as sweets. It was dynastic rivalries that caused Farouk to be separated from other members of his family this resulting in him growing up a lonely shy boy. At the age of 15 it was decided prince Farouk should be sent to England to continue his education.

After a tearful farewell to his mother Queen Nazly and his sisters, Farouk was despatched to the Royal Military Academy at Woolwich to study gunnery. At Woolwich life was not unpleasant he was spared the normal rigours of barrack room life and worst deprecations of the drill instructors. It was decided that he would be allowed to live out, and continue the luxury he had enjoyed all his life.

Kenry House Richmond was rented and he was able to set up a household with his military tutor General Aziz and Sir Ahmed Hassanien a worldly old Oxonian Diplomat, who was an attractive man with an irresistible appeal to the ladies. Hassanien encouraged the young prince in his pleasure seeking. The nocturnal pleasures of the young prince were indulged to the full.

General Aziz on the other hand was very upset by the conduct of the prince and this resulted in him sending a very critical report of Farouk to his father King Faud. With the report he submitted his resignation, ----which was accepted. General Aziz was later to become mentor of many young army officers including Gamal Abel Nasser.

The handsome young prince represented his father at the funeral of King George the V, and struck up a friendship with the new King Edward the VII. By 1936 Farouk had returned to Egypt and had fallen in love with a pretty vivacious girl who was to become Queen Farida. She was well able to use her feminine allures to capture the naïve young monarch. There is no doubt that Farouk fell head over heels in love with her. Egypt was destined to have a good looking King, a beautiful Queen, both supported by a still beautiful Queen Nazly.

Queen Nazly had chosen the wife for her son and all looked fair for the future of the monarchy. To largely illiterate country they were god like figures. After a dazzling wedding the royal couple settled down to a series of spectacular parties. The lawns and flower beds of the Koubbeh Palace were illuminated by thousands of coloured lights to form an enchanted background for the rich and privileged. Among the characters to appear among the party people, was none other than Donald Mac Lean with his American wife Melinda. They had become part of King Farouk's sister Faiza's group. The long round of pleasure could not go on for ever without a price being paid. Those who surrounded King Farouk placed their own ambitions above King and country, and fought hard to keep away from the King anyone who was not in agreement with any of his actions. The King was not a strong enough character to see through these deceptions. He was wise enough to seek out unbiased opinions.

The 1948 war against Israel was lost by a combination of the ineptitude of the Egyption Generals and the unreliability of her Arab Allies. King Farouk as the head of State had to bear the brunt of the recrimination. The Egyptians ran out of ammunition before they reached Gaza at the beginning of the war.

They had expected to defeat an unprofessional army of settlers who were ill equipped, with a few bayonet charges. They did not appreciate that the shrewd Jews would dig in and shoot the down from entrenched positions.

They look in vain for strong leadership. By 1951 the country was in a state of chaos, the Wafdist government were determined to get the British out of the Canal Zone. King Farouk even asked the British through an intermediary if they would defend him if things got out of control in Cairo.

Things came to a head in January 1952 when the police in Cairo went on strike and the good citizens went on a burning and looting spree. The Egyption government did nothing.

King Farouk was entertaining Army Officers to a banquet in the Abdin palace, they watched the flames of Cairo burning through the palace windows. Farouk waited until 4o'clock in the afternoon before ordering the army in to try and restore order.

This lost King Farouk the support of the officer corp, whose main aim now was to rid themselves of their inaffective King.

On the 26 July 1952 King Farouk abdicated, and was given another farewell from two of his sisters the Princesses Fawzia and Faiza as he sailed off in the Royal Yacht into exile.

The officers had got rid of the King, now they had to get rid of the British.

## Chapter 7

## INTRIGUE.PASSION & THE POWER OF SEX.

During the dance to promote Anglo American friendship Olga had struck up a friendship with a very odd American service man, by the name of Russell Keldale, who was also employed as clerk at his base.

This man's sole interests in life were drinking, gambling, and liaisons with women. While this was not held against him, he was by common knowledge shifty, unreliable, and had failed to report for duty on more than one occasion, leaving his colleagues to cover for him.

Sergeant Russell Keldale's prospects for advancement in the U.S. air force were very limited. He had no interests or hobbies except those mentioned and in consequence of these he was always short on money, and looking out for ways of making an extra 'buck' provided it did not require too much time away from his favourite pastimes.

There came about a subtle difference in the demeanour of Olga following her friendship with the American Sergeant.

In the Admin Office she seemed to be a little smugger and more confident in her general demeanour.  In fact there is a lively discussion about her change in attitude, the more basic airmen seemed the think that perhaps 'she was getting some'; but the more thoughtful amongst us thought it unlikely.

Olga had one or two occasions stated the fact that the men were only interested in one thing, and that once they had it they did not respect you. I believed at the time that she was probable right.

My information about Sgt Keldale came from my old school friend who I was in a habit of meeting for a drink in a local public house about once a month. Gerald Beaufoy had by now been promoted to sergeant.

.

Attached to our office were two civilian shorthand typists Norma and Kathleen who acted as secretaries to the Wing Commander. They were by any standard very intelligent and attractive girls. They also had one very big advantage over the women's Royal Air Force personnel. They would wear civilian clothes and this attire of smart skirts and blouses and other items of feminine adornment made then stand out like birds of paradise surrounded by uniformly attired sparrows.

Norma a natural blonde had the fair porcelain type of beauty that could not fail to attract men of all ages. Her creamy white skin belonged to dreams. Norma was so attractive that she could have made a 'Bishop kick a hole in a stained glass window', in order to gain her attention. She spoke with the soft Gloucestershire accent which again accentuated her appeal. Norma was engaged to married to local solicitor, and definitely out of bounds to the licentious airmen who surrounded her.

Kathleen her companion is a dark eyed, dark haired beauty, with a full and voluptuous figure. Kathleen had a bold look about her, and although she lacked the delicate features of her colleague she did not suffer from any scarcity of attention. The Wing Commander kept these two near to himself and the opportunity to fraternise with them was very limited.

However the day arrived when due to some reorganisation in their office the word came down from on high that our assistance would be required to move some heavy filing cabinets, from the inner sanctum into the secretary's office. Having been detailed to do the job by the Warrant

Officer I reported to the Wing Commander. “Carry on corporal, Miss Browne will show you what needs doing," that was all the conversation I had with the 'Winco'.

After an exchange of pleasantries, with Kathleen Brown and the blond goddess I took my jacket off and got to work moving the furniture around in accordance with their instructions. It was a pleasant interlude from working with all service personnel. The girls thanked me for my efforts and I left their office with a warm glow. It was heady stuff to be appreciated by these two very attractive girls.

A few days later I received a telephone call from Kathleen Brown asking me to go back to their office. There was another job to be done. I went to the office and to my surprise I was shown in to the Wing Commanders office.

"Where is the Wing Commander?" I asked. "He has gone to a conference with the Group Captain at the camp and he has taken Norma with him to take the minutes of the meeting,” she replied.

Kathleen sat in the Wing Commanders chair and leant back showing a long expanse of black silk stocking." Sit down Jack no one will come in here without first telephoning." My nervousness at being in the inner sanctum must have shown itself for she said "Why are you fidgeting on the seat?"

Sitting opposite this glamorous figure who was herself crossing and uncrossing her legs with un-nerving regularity was an unfair question to put to a young eighteen year old man.

"I have been thinking about you for some time” she said.

Our eyes met, and her coal black eyes transmitted an invitation that even an inexperienced youth could not mistake. Kathleen beckoned me over to the Wing Commanders Chair. "Would you like to kiss me?" There could only be one answer.

I kissed her with passionate surprise.

"That's it; that's wonderful" she said. Encouraged by her

I kissed her on the mouth and neck.

In a moment my hands were all over her lovely body.

The frenzied appetite of a young animal had been aroused.

"Why not do it to me?" she said, her breathing growing more and more rapid.

Never before had I experienced such intensity of pleasure.

"You've enjoyed yourself," she said, with a sly knowing smile.

" Yes" I replied," with complete honesty and gratitude, "You've taught me a lot"

Like my first solo flight in an aeroplane; this was an experience that I would never be forgotten.

From that day I have always admired women with a gentle nature and a warm body. When I left her in the office to return to my section I extracted a promise from her to contact me again when the opportunity presented itself.

Back in my all service atmosphere I was glad when the time arrived to be transported back to the main camp for our tea at the end of the day's work. While riding on the trooper back to camp, I was brought down to earth by the raucous singing of some women's Royal Air Force personnel singing in the back of another truck "Stand by your beds, here comes the Air vice Marshall he's got lots of rings, but he's only got one Arsehole." Perhaps I was ultra-sensitive to the crudity of the ditty, but to this day I have always disliked coarse language especialy by women.

Back at camp the pleasures of the afternoon faded to the back of my mind , when I recalled the offer of a Court Martial if I had not accepted the subordinate commanders punishment of three days confined to camp, and the loss of a day's pay, for coming back from a week-end pass seven minutes late.

What punishment would they have inflicted on me had I been caught 'flagrante delecto ' with the Wing Commanders secretary, not only in his office, but on his desk?

The pretty, vivacious Kathleen was well able to wield the feminine wiles and flirtations to achieve her ambitions. The naive and unsophisticated Corporal must have been an easy conquest.

To the astonishment of not only of the section in which she worked, but to the twenty other members of the WRAF with whom she shared a billet Olga appeared one day wearing an obviously expensive engagement ring. Olga announced she was engaged to be married to an American serviceman. The gregarious Thelma congratulated her with all the sincerity that could be raised by another woman who had experienced several engagements that had been short lived.

The men in the section just could not understand how the surly Olga had managed to achieve this status, but they agreed that some Americans would jump anything that stood still long enough.

On being questioned as to her future, Olga said "Russell had to sort out some paper work because he needed to get permission to get married." We knew that potential brides of American service men had to be vetted before they married, because entry into the USA was subject to good character and health.

However we all wished her well and hoped for the replacement typist to be comparable to one of the Wing Commanders secretaries.

We were to be involved fairly quickly in the complications that followed the unlikely attachment of a dour English RAF typist, with the personality of a rasp, and a characterless bird brained American sergeant.

The impecunious Sergeant Keldale evidently had delusions of grandeur and he decided to approach the KGB and offer to sell them information. The problem was that he had no idea of how to contact the Russians. Sgt Russell Keldale had served in Berlin before being posted to England, so he decided to take his leave in Germany and approach the Russians in their sector of the city. He set out and arrived in the Karl horst district of the city and presented himself to the Soviet officials there.

A stern faced official told him "We have no time for traitors or parasites in the Soviet Union, we are working for peace and world socialism" "However if you really have useful information or can obtain it, we will arrange for an interview with the KGB." Sgt Keldale assured them he could obtain useful information for them.

Sgt Keldale was then told that he would be met at the railways station the next day at 11AM for a further interview.

The next morning he met by two KGB officers one a big granite faced man, the other a stocky man who looked a bit like an over-worked schoolmaster. They drove him to a massive house built of stone, with the heavily shuttered windows.

When they entered the house there was a third man sitting at a large table in the middle of the room. Without saying a word the man filled four glasses with vodka and raised his glass and then said "Peace Comrades.

"We have been told you want to help the cause of world socialism is that true?"

"Well I don't know a lot about it"

"Why do you want to help us?"

"Well I am fed up with the Air force"

"Well a lot of men get fed up with being in the service, but they do not become traitors to their country."

"Well I am in a position to supply you with a lot of useful information."

The officers kept filling his glass with vodka while they questioned him about his military experience and his duties. They did not seem over impressed with his record or his potential.

However when he mentioned that he had an English girl friend who worked at the Record Office of the RAF they pricked up their ears. Then he said, he could, obtain confidential lists of postings of airmen who were to witness the Atomic bomb tests that were to take place shortly.

This pearl of information, even if it came from a drunken swine, could be useful propaganda even if not of any great strategic value. The postings of young servicemen to see how they were affected by nuclear explosions was a highly contentious issue. Large demonstrations were being organised to protest about the continuing tests of nuclear bombs and the 'Ban the Bomb' campaign was in full flow in the UK and elsewhere in the world.

Although Keldale would not be in a position to communicate information on the scale of a Burgess or Maclean even a lowly man could become a 'sleeper' and useful in the years to come.

For the KGB being in the process of building its own empire within the USSR, every recruit living in the west could be a potential source of information. The interviewing officer's promised nothing but offered to talk to him again in a few weeks' time in either London or Birmingham.

Colonel Cupric gave him $200 in a plain brown envelope, a password, and a sign by which he would recognise his contact. The password would always be contained in a sentence.

"The password is 'Eagle'. Is that clear? Asked Colonel Cupric.

"Yes Sir. How will I know my contact?"

"You won't we will contact you, and during the conversation he will say that the eagle is a fine bird.

You will reply especially on a ten dollar coin, is that clear? "

“Yes Sir."

"The sign will be that your contact will be carrying a folded copy of the Times.

Is that clear?"

"Yes Sir."

Colonel Yuri Cupric was not very impressed, with the brightness or perception of the new comrade. Keldale returned to his unit excited at the easy was he had earned two hundreds 'bucks'. Keldale decided the next thing was to do was to advance his relationship with Olga.

He had been married before in Germany, but there would be no need to tell his little English sweet heart, he prided himself that he had a way with the 'broads'.

Keldale invested $100 in a diamond ring.

About two months later the Adjutant summoned me into his office and told me that the Wing Commander and an officer from the special investigations branch would want to interview me during the course of the next few days. The first thing that came to mind was that somehow the Winco had found out about my dalliance with his secretary and that I was about to pay the penalty for my few minutes pleasure. I felt sure it was going to be the glasshouse for me, I had heard all about the horrors of a military prison and I started to literally quake in my shoes.

The military still shot people for treason and hanging was the penalty for murder.

My extreme agitation must have shown because the old boy said "Don't worry Corporal I will be in there with you"

"Can I ask what is about? Am I on a charge Sir, if so what am I charged with? "

"I am not allowed to tell you Corporal it is top secret and you must not discuss even this interview with anyone."

This left me to sweat for a couple of days, two very long days.

Meanwhile it was common knowledge that there had been some irregularities during one of the night shifts involving a corporal and a member of the women's Royal Air Force that had resulted in the women having the words TOP SECRET stamped on her stomach just above that area that was indeed top secret for most women.

The woman concerned had not complained herself and had joined in the horseplay with enthusiasm so the camp grape vine reported.

Who had been present at this incident?

Who had been vindictive enough to want to report this?

These were two of the questions that needed answering to satisfy the curiosity of the camp, an RAF camp at this time being like a small village that needed a certain **amountof intrigue *and gossip to smooth the wheels of everyday life.***

The woman that had been stamped was the irrepressible Thelma.

Thelma would not have got anyone into trouble she was easy going to the extreme and always avoided trouble. The waspish Olga pointed out that the stamp was inappropriate for her anyway. No one knew the name of the informant.

The RAF in common with all services did their best to keep their personnel healthy in body. In this respect all ranks were obliged to attend for FFI parades, these initials standing for ‘free from infection’. All airmen could be issued with 'rubber overcoats' as contraceptives were known at the time, so there was no real excuse for catching a sexually transmitted disease. The dread of catching clap and having the knob drop off was enough was enough to deter most young men from casual sex. There was a lot of fear and a great lack of knowledge on the subject among young people. Some of the information available was so horrific that it is surprising that the next generation were conceived at all.

One airman on parade for the normal cursory inspection did have a problem. The Medical officer looked at him and saw the limp weeping specimen that was produced for him to inspect." I think it's got a cold “said the airman rather sheepishly.” Very well airman we will give it a minute to see if it sneezes, and if it doesn't we will call it gonorrhoea “said the MO without blinking an eyelid.

On another occasion the medical officer was a little dumpy middle aged woman, we all stood in a row facing her with our trousers lowered to half-mast.

The lady approached each man in turn as she proceeded at a sedate pace along the row of young men. Just as she arrived in front of one young man the instrument she was to inspect started to rise. "There will be none of that” she said firmly and tapped the offending organ with the end of her pencil. Much to our surprise she smiled and went merrily on her on her way, an example of a sensible self-possessed professional woman with a sense of humour.

The comment of the accompanying NCO to his squad to "clear off you lot of lecherous perverts” being delivered for once I suspect with-out malice.

The memorable morning arrived and I accompanied the Flt Lt into the Wing Commanders office. The pressure was off because there was no accused and escort routine that accompanied any disciplinary procedure.

Just what it was all about I was to learn a little later.

The Wing Commander motioned for me to stand in front of his desk, this being officially only the second time that I had been in his office with him. Seated behind the desk were two men in civilian clothes. Both men were obviously men of rank and influence because the adjutant addressed them both as Sir.

In front of the desk were two chairs the Wing Commander introduced the adjutant to the men. One was a colonel in the American Air force and the other a Wing Commander from our special investigation branch.

By now I was blanching visible. Corporals just did not get into the presence of such high brass without there being something very out of the ordinary, normally unpleasant in store for them.

The Wing Commander spoke to me " I expect you are wonder wondering what this is all about Corporal. It concerns a young lady." I immediately felt faint and thought I was going to pass out.

"We want to know if you can help us in respect of a confidential matter it concerns LACW Olga Newcastle."

The sense of relief that I experienced was so great that I thought I was experiencing a miracle. Thank you God I thought once again. The next miracle followed the Wing Commander introduced me to the two officers who were sitting with him at the Desk.

The one rose to greet me. He was tall very straight backed, with a very full head of hair, and wearing a small dark moustache a handsome man. "Dan Davies nice to meet you" He shook my hand.

"Sit down I would like to talk to you."

'Sit down' this was almost unheard of, certainly in my experience.

It was the American Colonel who had spoken first to me .

The pause caused by my slight hesitation in sitting was filled by the other British officer who said in a brusque but friendly enough manner

"Sit down Corporal, or are you waiting for a Royal invitation."

The adjutant and I sat down side by side in front of these impressive men.

The atmosphere relaxed and the American asked " Will you help us with our enquires?"

"Yes Sir, if I can" but I was at a loss to know how Olga Newcastle and I fitted into any enquires that they were making.

He looked at a file on the desk and said “Do you know Sergeant Gerald Beaufoy?

"Yes we were at school together. I hope he is not in any trouble? "

"Just reply to the question Corporal “interjected the British Officer who I then twigged was a lawyer, from my twice weekly attendance at the cinema during my young adult life.

“A fair question" said the American continuing “Sergeant Beaufoy is assisting us with the case in hand and because of your friendship with him I am hoping you will help us in a similar manner."

The friendly manner of the American and the fact that he did not talk down to me endeared him to me immediately. I looked at the adjutant for in the hierarchical set up of the armed forces English Corporals did not make promises even to American Colonels without the permission of their superior officer.

This created the moment that the Flight Lieutenant Admin was waiting for. He cleared his throat and started on a long monologue to the effect that anything the Administrative Section could do to help our allies would receive his fullest support and co-operation.

The Colonel thus assured of his support and the fact that I was not indispensable to the efficient running of the Record Office, and could be spared to help in any way that would be required, thanked him for his co-operation.

The tall American continued “Are you aware that one of your colleagues Olga Newcastle is courting one of our airmen.” I was a little puzzled by the question but very relieved that the name of the Winco's secretary had not featured in any of the conversations.

“Yes Sir, I think the whole camp knows about it."

The accountant Wing Commander looked up at me and glared. The lawyer Wing Commander stared at me but said nothing.

"The man we are concerned about is Sgt Keldale and we believe that he may be engaged in espionage, our man involved in keeping tabs on him is Gerald Beaufoy. We may want you to help, by assisting him to keep track of any suspicious activities involving Olga Newcastle and Sgt Keldale.

We would want you to look listen and observe them. Do nothing but report anything no matter how trivial that does not fit in with the normal pattern of work undertaken by them.

Report to Flt Lieutenant Whitehead in the first instance” The adjutant fairly glowed with importance at what must have been an exciting event in his career.

I replied that I would do my best and the Colonel thanked me and in a daze I was led outside into the Adjutants Office. On the basis of the good reception we had received, once we were out of the Wing Commanders Flt Lieutenant Whitehead confided in me that the Wing Commander did not know anything about Olga being engaged to an American Airman. Indeed it would not under normal circumstances come to the notice of a senior officer.

"Your comment Corporal about all the camp knowing was not appreciated by him."

In the effluent again I thought." Be very cautious what you say Corporal, the other officer is a lawyer." This proved to be very good advice and confirmed my guess regarding the profession of the second Wing Commander.

I was again cautioned not to reveal anything of this to any one and returned to work. The Adjutant put out a story that I was being considered for promotion, and it was accepted that 'the snotty nosed corporal was just the type to be trained up to be a bleeding officer'.

## CHAPTER 8.

## SPECIAL DUTIES

The possession of two stripes came fairly easily, to Keith Smart and me but to some of the old sweats two or more stripes were the result of years of service. A quick promotion for a smart arse did produce some resentment among some of the longer serving airmen. The best part for me was that I had my own small room at the end of the billet so that I did enjoy an element of privacy with the status of being a non-commissioned officer also came the exemption from fatigues, and the privilege of being thought capable of thinking.

In the RAF of the early 1950's most of the airmen had left school at fourteen years of age and those fortunate enough to have been educated to the age of sixteen had a very distinct advantage. The majority of boys laboured in unskilled trades and were in the main the best paid initially. The next group became apprentices and learnt a skilled trade, existing on very little money but with the satisfaction of knowing that they would eventually become craftsmen and 'always have a trade to fall back on'. They would eventually earn good money and have a good standard of living. These being generally called the blue collar workers.

The other group consisted of the so called white collar workers who were looked down on by the blue collar workers.

How could you consider yourself a worker with lily white hands?

My father again had instilled in me that I would not make any real money by getting my hands dirty so having always been taught to obey parents and governors and lacking any real practical skills I elected to be a white collar worker.

The great opportunities presented by the forces to train men and women in different skills became more obvious to me. The air force itself required ground skills as far ranging as air-frame mechanics, armourers, cooks, clerks, dental workers, medical assistants, typists, parachute packers, drivers, draughtsmen, even men skilled in handling small boats and interpreters. The list being almost endless all these trades and more being required to support the crème de la crème, the aircrew who were our ‘raison de etre'.

The overwhelming fear at this time being the strength of the Soviet Union and her Allies, kindly Uncle Joe Stalin and our heroic Russian brothers of a few years ago, had now become Dictator Stalin the Russian bear and his hostile cubs. The communists were hell bent on the course of converting the world to their way of doing things.

The serviceman knew that it was not for him to reason why but to follow orders.

The average serviceman still accepted without question that his was not to reason why, but the willingness to die on some foreign field for some transient foreign policy did not have the same unquestioning acceptance given by previous generations. The rank and file were better informed, and were more selective when assessing the risks of any particular strategy.

For too long it had been true in a military sense that we were a nation of lions led by asses.

The only compensation being that other countries were in the main even worse led than we were.

A few weeks working in the office it became very clear that relations between the two women were wearing a bit thin, I had by now become something of a mentor to the flighty Thelma.

During a temporary absence of the dour Olga Thelma asked "Is it right Corporal that they will not let communists into the United States?"

"You could not be more correct "I replied.

"How is it that Olga is going to marry Russell Keldale and go and live there?"

"If she is a communist and it is found out by the authorities she would certainly be banned from going there, but if she keeps her mouth shut no one will know."

"It's not fair although I can't prove it I reckon she shopped me over the lark with the TOP SECRET stamp. Corporal Stanley Bunker is in trouble and so am I. It really is no business of any one but ourselves, we were not hurting anybody"

"Can I ask you a question Thelma; was there any person present other than Stanley Bunker and yourself when the stamping took place?"

"No there was not. What do you think I am a pervert? "

"Well if there was no one else present how would they know that you had been stamped? Could Olga have seen you in the bathhouse or the toilet or did you tell anyone, as you said it was only a bit of fun?"

"No I do not let other women see me what do you think I am a lesbian?"

"No Thelma I am just trying to find out for you who could possibly have been in the position to see such a private mark."

"I think that bitch Olga had something to do with it. I have not seen Stanley since this happened and I think he is avoiding me."

"Well Thelma if I hear anything I will let you know, but I will not say anything unless I am sure that what I hear is correct.

What made you ask about Olga? She is only engaged and you know that many things can happen between an engagement and a wedding."

"Well she has applied for a week's leave and instead of going to her sisters in Yorkshire, where she always goes; she has given her address as a hotel in Birmingham. You come from there don't you?"

"Yes" Where is she staying?

"The Victoria Hotel."

I knew it all right; you needed to be very well off to stay there.

This was interesting because all WRAF passes were issued through their own administration section and although we would be aware that she was on leave we would not know where she was going.

"I think she is having a dirty weekend with that American, and she has gone and spoiled my friendship with Stanley"

I offered my sympathy to Thelma and said that you normally harvested what you sowed, so that Olga would not benefit in the long run from her spiteful behaviour.

I also said “If Stanley is worth having he would be in touch soon and if he did not bother it would be a sign that they were not really cut out for each other.

I know you are popular Thelma so just carry on as if nothing has happened."

I then passed on this information to the adjutant, reminding him that Gerald Beaufoy and I had intensive knowledge of Birmingham and its surroundings.

A few days later I was told that I was to accompany Flt Llt Whitehead to the American Air force Camp.

We arrived at the American Air in an official RAF staff car I occupied one of the front seats with the RAF driver while Flt Llt Whitehead sat in state in the back of the car clutching an imposing brown leather brief case. We had our identity checked by a giant of an American policeman, and received a smart salute and were directed towards the officers club. We had been instructed to see Colonel Dan Davies wearing civilian clothing; it felt good even if the salute was only in my case reflected glory. We were shown into what seemed to be a comfortable study cum lounge. Seated at the end of the room behind a large desk was the tall dark haired American Colonel whom I had met earlier. Sitting a desk placed at right angles to him was a familiar figure. As we walked down the room the American came from behind the desk and walked towards us.

"Thank you very much for coming hear so promptly I have something to show you that may be of great importance to both our countries. I want to address you both by your civilian titles or Christian names whichever is appropriate at the time

I want you to call me Dan, and this is Gerald" he said introducing Gerald Beaufoy to Flt Llt Whitehead.

"Pleased to meet you Sir" said my old school friend "My name is Gerald, what I call you?"

“John " said the rather taken aback Adjutant.  I could not feel how I could call him John, so I decided mentally just to omit the Sir while we were with the Americans.

"Does the 10th of May 1953    mean anything to you?"  "Why yes" said the Flt Llt who had been reading up his notes for most of the journey to the meeting.  "That is the date that LACW Olga Newcastle has booked to go on leave."

"That date is also the date that our Sergeant Russell Keldale has booked to go on leave."

"Do you think they have an assignation?"  Asked the wide eyed Admin Officer.

"You bet your sweet ass" Replied the Colonel without a moment’s hesitation.

"The address the sergeant has put on his leave pass is the Victoria Hotel Birmingham.”

The Colonel now produced a photograph of a middle aged granite faced man. "Do you know who this is?”  The man was in uniform and wearing the rank markings of a full Colonel in the USSR army.

"No Sir" said John and I almost in the same breath.

A slight frown from our own American ally brought the correction "Sorry Dan” from our worthy Adjutant.

"This man is Colonel Yuri Cupric of the KGB. Officially he is attached to the Soviet Trade Mission in London. He only flew into England a few days ago, and he is booked in to the Victoria Hotel with the Trade mission for three days.

This covers the period that Olga Newcastle and Sergeant Russell Keldale are staying there.

This is highly suspicious because Keldale is always hard up for money and rooms at the Victoria are not cheap. We have checked and the rooms have been paid for cash in advance. The cost of the rooms would be equal to about a month's pay for a top sergeant. What I am proposing is that Gerald Beaufoy and Jack Darby keep observations on them on them to see if Colonel Cupric or any of his staff get in touch with either Olga Newcastle or Sgt Keldale.

For this purpose we have booked the suite opposite to the one the Sergeant and his friend will occupy. The door of this suite is equipped with a spy hole so you will be able to see any one going in or out of their suite. It also has the advantage that it is a corner suite and has a common wall with the one they will be occupying We will install some recording equipment that will be monitored by Gerald Beaufoy who is an expert in these matters.

We have cleared this operation with your authorities. I do not have to tell you how delicate these matters are we aim to keep the so called cold war ------cold.

Mr Churchill is trying to arrange a meeting between President Eisenhower and the Soviet leaders at the moment. President Eisenhower said, 'He regards Britain as his principal ally' when talking to your foreign Secretary Anthony Eden about the possible use of atomic bombs in the conflicts in which you are currently engaged. I have just heard the Ike has had to rebuke Mr Churchill for suggesting that they meet next time in Moscow. We speak from strength we will dictate to those commy bastards where and when we meet!"

There was no denying that the man spoke with all the confidence of a representative of the most powerful nation on earth.

"Jack can brief Gerald on all he knows about Olga Newcastle.

Gerald can brief Jack on Keldale".

I suggest we break for lunch then the young men can get their heads together over the details of their task. Is that OK with you John? "

"Certainly, yes Dan" replied the Admin officer.

Things were moving quickly and differently for both of us.

The 2nd June 1953 had been the most important date in the minds of the English contingent up to this point in time. We had been practising and enduring extra drill for months in preparation for the Coronation of her Majesty Queen Elizabeth the 11, following the death of King George VI her father during the morning of the 6th February 1952.

We had seen The Queen return to London from Kenya the following day to be greeted by Mr Winston Churchill and the assembled politicians at the foot of the steps to the aeroplane.

We were not to know that Mount Everest had been climbed for the first time by Edmund Hilary and Tenzing Norgay members of a Commonwealth team led by Colonel John Hunt. The news of this success was to be announced on Coronation day the 2nd of June 1953.

The 10th of May was only three weeks away and we were instructed to visit the Victoria Hotel and familiarise ourselves with the layout of the Hotel and the immediate vicinity, as soon as possible. The Colonel requested that I be relieved of my present duties in order to concentrate on the mission in hand.

This was accomplished by inventing a linguist course that required me to travel in civilian clothing from the camp every day. My presence at my old place of work to report to the Adjutant was therefore not the subject of speculation. Many servicemen attended language courses, one of the perks being that they could often land cushy numbers with one of our military attaches attached to one of our Embassies abroad.

I was now beginning to enjoy the game. Like most young men my sartorial knowledge and experience had been very limited, one suit for work, and a sports coat and grey flannels for leisure, being the limit of my wardrobe. There was not a lot of choice available.

If as I did, you rejected the dress of the Teddy boy who wore single-breasted suits with narrow lapels, narrow pegged top trousers and 'brothel creepers',which were big ugly shoes with soles made of crepe rubber at least three inches thick.

Colonel Dan Davies decreed that Gerald Beaufoy and I should be equipped with new clothing that would enable us to mix in the crowd of business men who would stay at a first class hotel, This seemed to be too good to be true, but we were despatched to a gentlemen's outfitters and kitted out with the best quality clothing I had ever worn in my life.

We would be earning these clothes in due course but the euphoria at that moment years of during clothes rationing was another experience that I enjoyed for the first time.

## CHAPTER 9.

## CABARET & GUNS.

The British nuclear programme had now been publicly admitted for the first time, having been unveiled with the atomic rocket testing at Woomera in northern Australia in 1952. Mr Churchill was now pressing on with the even more deadly hydrogen bomb programme. This caused great public fear and the moral dilemma that was presented by these horrendous forces of mass destruction was very much on every ones minds.

In 1953 the American CIA achieved the fortunate deposition of Mussadiq as Prime Minister of Persia.

Allen Dulles's operation 'Ajax' achieved the return of the Shah to the peacock throne.

British servicemen were being posted to Libya, Jordan, and the Persian Gulf. There being a great need to protect our oil interests. The general feeling being that a combined American British presence would help stabilise the region and ensure our vital oil supplies.

The Russians of course had a vested interest in de-stabilising the area, chaos being the best breeding ground for the spread of the gospel of communism.

I was also concerned because my younger brother serving in the RAF Regiment in Kenya was having a rough time due to Mau-Mau out-break among the Kikuya tribe; this state of emergency would eventually lead to the loss of 10,000 African and European lives.

With fighting continuing in Malaya and trouble looming in Cyprus and Guyana there were many dangerous posting available for the British serviceman.

The prospect of doing undercover work to help defeat the spread of communism was very attractive in particular if this could be done in comfortable surroundings

On the 9th of May Geoffrey Beaufoy arrived at my camp in a smart Sunbeam Talbot coupe to collect me to go on our mission. "Part of our cover, Uncle Sam's paying." said Geoffrey.

The height of ambition for most young men at this time would have been to drive a new Ford popular available in any colour provided it was in black.

We took our time and motored through the pleasant rich Gloucestershire country side, passing Chosen Hill where enthusiastic young men chased "rounds of cheese down the hill "to win the acclaim of local girls, or in many cases a broken or fractured arm or leg.

We skirted just south of Cheltenham to visit Leckhampton Hill one of the most dramatic places in Gloucestershire and the site of one of the finest Cotswold Iron age forts. Nearby I wanted to show Gerald the Devil's Chimney. This is a slender peculiarly shaped limestone rock, 50 feet high; according to local superstition it rises straight from hell. Its slim dramatic shape in fact is not a natural feature but is the result of centuries of quarrying around it.

We then went through the small town of Pershore this place is known as the capital of the plum, and is situated on land rich in corn and fruit production, to Birmingham the metropolis of the Midlands.

We passed the old Crown Inn in Digbeth which has stood on its spot since 1366 and had in its time hosted Queen Elizabeth 1.

We were about the business of young Queen Elizabeth 11 and we intend to give it our best shot. We checked into the Victoria Hotel and tried not to be overawed by the splendour of the marbled halls and the rich panelling of the public rooms.

The uniformed porters with their bright demeanour were in most cases ex-service men who were only to please to throw up salutes to the two smart looking men who drove up in a new Sunbeam car; they arranged to take our bags to our rooms. The appropriate tip was offered and received with equal courtesy. The offer on the part of the older of the porters to obtain 'anything you young gentlemen should require' was noted with thanks.

Once we had settled into the room and found that everything had been provided as promised we went down into the dining room and found that a small table had been reserved for us well out of view of the main dining area. We would have a clear uninterrupted view of the dinners in the main body of the dining room.

We enjoyed the diner menu of crème of celery soup, followed by roast veal and stuffing accompanied by Brussels sprouts, peas baked potatoes and creamed potatoes. This was followed by apple tart with custard, and cheese and biscuits. To finish the meal we had coffee and a brandy. The meal had been supported by a good bottle of claret. By looking at the menu card I could see that the meal had cost more than I earned in a week.

I had enjoyed the meal even more because it had been made clear by Colonel Dan Davies that the expenses would be picked up by the US government. I felt that John Whitehead would have been green with envy had he witnessed the luxury that we were now enjoying.

The fact that there is no such thing as a free dinner was as yet an unknown truth in my experience.

After dinner we drifted into the bar feeling well pleased with the world.

Gerald said "Why do we not try a night club while we have a chance?"

"Why not I have never been in a night club"

We consulted our friendly porter who with a knowing wink gave us a card and directed us to a Cabaret Club within easy walking distance of the hotel.

We enjoyed the stroll through the well light safe streets to the Club. On arrival we found that we had to ring a bell to gain admittance. The door was opened by a large man wearing a dress suit who looked exactly what he was, an ex-boxer, he had a very quiet gentle voice but it clearly indicated that you did not take liberties with him.

On presenting the card we were immediately treated like visiting royalty.

We were told to go to the top of the red plush staircase where we would be met by our hostess. We were met by a charming lady in evening dress who escorted us to the bar. In front of the bar was a small circular dance floor with tables around it. We were charged about the same as we had paid for dinner and told that we could enjoy the cabaret with two drinks compliments of the house. During the time the cabaret was not performing we would be able to dance with the young ladies who were decorating the sides of the dance floor

We could not help observing that the men present in the room all seemed to be either in uniform or considerably older than the girls in the room. We had a drink while waiting for the cabaret.

I said to one of the girls "Would you like to dance? "I will if you like but I would rather have a gin and tonic." This ungracious remark was accepted by me and I bought the girl her gin and tonic which she downed in the twinkling of an eye.

She then sat fingering the glass and all but asking for a refill. I said "Do you work at this club?" "Yes" she replied we are hostesses, we get paid commission on all the drinks you buy us."

Well that's honest I thought. "Do you want another drink?" "Yes please, gin and tonic."

A small dark man now stepped forward and announced the cabaret, "Miss Dolores Smith and the story of the wicked shoe maker." A small stool had been placed in the centre of the dance floor and a heavily made up man was sitting on the stool supposedly mending a pair of slippers.

A woman even more heavily made up appeared wearing a flowing dress and very little else. The dark man intoned that poor Dolores was an orphan who depended on her shoes to make her living dancing in the streets to earn a few pennies.

There was not a single tear shed by the audience.

The woman started to say that she had come for her shoes, but had not the money to pay for the repair. "Oh what can I do? Oh what can I do? Oh what can I do?"

A member of the audience yelled "Get F.....d and quick about it. I've a train to catch, this raucous comment being received by the audience with a cheer.

The wicked shoe maker suggested that she give herself to him on the table...... This she says she is unwilling to do but she will dance for him as payment for the shoe repair, if he is not satisfied she will come back the next night and dance again for him.

This the shoemaker agrees to. She throws of the dress to reveal that she just wearing a G string, and two sequins, one on each breast. Dolores dances around giving the dance her all, displaying enough of her charms to satisfy the curiosity of most of the audience. After a while the wicked shoe maker reneges on his bargain and chases Dolores around the stage and in and out of the tables and chairs.

After a chase the shoe maker, himself dressed in tights with a suspiciously large bulge in the crutch area catches Dolores, bends her over the table and appears to have his way with her. The lights go out momentarily and when they come one again Dolores and the wicked shoe maker have disappeared.

The little dark man re-appears and said “Part two of this drama will be staged in about one hours’ time, the bar is open drink up and enjoy yourselves”

We decided it was time we had a dance so we asked the two girls we had been sitting with to dance. For my part the dance was less than exciting and I was pleased to sit down again. The girl Sheila asked for another gin and tonic stating that she could not sit with us unless we were buying drinks.

We purchased another round of drinks and asked the girls how they came to work here. "Why it is warm and pleasant and we get to meet men."

"What did you do before you worked here” I asked” Oh I was on the game” she replied “When did you give it up?"

"Last night" was the reply.

"I finish here at midnight you can see me home if you like.

It will cost you a fiver but it will be worth it,"

"Sorry no offence but we have a full day tomorrow."

"We get some very high class men in here we are expecting a lot of foreign men in tomorrow, so we will be busy you have your chance tonight"

"No thanks."

"Time wasting sod, I suppose you and your friend had better be getting off together."

With this and a sneer she flounced off.

Cheeky cow I thought.

I was beginning to learn.

Gerald Beaufoy on the other hand seemed to be getting on very well with a petite blond girl. The girl had large blue eyes and an air of innocence that did not appear to me, to have much in common with her occupation as a hostess. The girl seemed to be captivated by Gerald and I put it down partly to his American accent.

"Samantha is working here while she is studying to be an actress, I am going home with her after the show I think she may be able to help us. If you want to go back to the hotel I will see you in the morning Jack."

After our long day I was only to please to stroll back to the hotel, I had not got the stamina or the experience of either Gerald or the man in tights.

In fact I was feeling a little guilty at going to the Cabaret Club and wonders how many sins I had committed that night either in thought or deed. With so much suffering in the world and such a shortage of food I felt sure that I was guilty of the sin of gluttony and even drunkenness. Lust was a sin that I had been tempted with, but even with a mind less than clear I felt that it was not right to pay for sex, I had at least avoided that sin.

Having received a Christian upbringing I was to find that in times of real danger that this faith meant the difference between survival and defeat, the real problem being this feeling of guilt that was produced when committing minor sins. Many things would have to be done in the line of duty and if on later reflection it was not a pleasure then perhaps it was not a sin either. As a priest might say "It is only a sin if you enjoyed it."

Gerald had no religious inhibitions, and I felt that there was something missing in his makeup. His attitude being that we are here today to enjoy life and to make the best of every opportunity. This is not a rehearsal for life. Today is your life being his philosophy.

There is something very cold and deadly in his character which I cannot understand, at times he gives the impression of having looked over the wall at death and returned determined not to miss any experience on the remainder of his mortal journey.

I had been surprised to see that under his coat in a shoulder holster Gerald carried an automatic pistol. “I carry this pistol with the authority of both our governments. I hope we do not need it, but we have to be prepared for any eventuality" was the chilling reply I got to my enquiry as to whether this was necessary.

The next morning we set up our surveillance equipment and waited for the arrival of Russell Keldale and his fiancée Olga. We were rewarded by the arrival of the pair of them during the afternoon. At first I had misgivings about listening in on the private conversations of the couple. The reception through the headphones was crystal clear we could hear everything that was said in the room.

“I am going to have a bath” said Olga “I'll join you” “You won’t, be patient you won’t lose out.”

“O K babe"

"Do not call me babe"

“OK Olga.

Room service this is Mr Keldale will you send up a bottle of vodka

and a bottle of orange, Room 301 charge it, OK."

After a while we saw the waiter arrive with the two bottles and guessed that Keldale would settle down with his bottle. After about twenty minutes we heard Olga say "You can have the bathroom now."

"Come here babe" "Do not call me babe; I am not having you near me until you have had a bath."

We heard the sharp intake of breath by the airman who must have been quite frustrated by now.

"How much have you had to drink? Half the bottle by the look of it, you are not coming near me until you have a bath.

Do I have to repeat myself again?

“We were quite impressed by the determined voice of Olga. We heard the bathroom door slam and everything went quiet. There was absolute silence for about an hour and we thought that they had fallen asleep after the rigours of their journey;

Suddenly there was as piecing shriek followed by the sound of several slaps. This was followed by rhythmic sound of two bodies banging together, the next sound we heard was Olga sobbing and screaming at Keldale.

"What are we going to do?" I asked Gerald "It sounds as if he is killing her, we cannot allow that to happen."

"Jack you are so naive some women get turned on by a bit of slapping around. Some guys need to slap a woman about to get aroused. Those two could be putting our two countries in danger. We will not interfere and blow our cover.

We are also not here to educate you about sex. If you are not up to the job tell me and I will have to make other arrangements." This did not sound like my old school mate talking.

"Jack I will level with you I am attached to military intelligence and we work very closely with the CIA and your intelligence service. We do not mess about, there is too much at stake you have some local knowledge that is useful to us and I thought you were the man to help us.

If you would rather be back filing in charts for your Wing Commander tell me before we get into this operation any further. I saw your face when you spotted the automatic. We are observing two people.

There is back up watching us, you know the telephone number we were given, if we need assistance we would have it within ten minutes by calling that number."

"Sorry Gerald I did not quite realise the importance of the task."

"Remember buddy I'm your immediate boss now and your passport for keeping out of trouble”.

By the way last night after you left that was primary business. I may need to use Samantha again; she has a flat that she shares with another girl a dancer.”

Over the head phones I heard Olga laughing and telling Keldale how wonderful he was.

Gerald looked at me with a kind of funny smile.

"Well I suppose it's whatever turns you on” I said.

“You are learning “he replied, but he seemed to have that half dead look in his eyes that betrayed no emotion.

Gerald did not have any shyness with young women; he had the social graces and the charm to develop relationships quickly. He was courteous and drank only in moderation, and he did not smoke. Gerald was a most eligible bachelor but I had not heard him talk of a regular girlfriend, or indeed of any special relationship.

At school we had sat next to each other, I was boxing champion for the year and at that time much harder than him. Some experience in life had now honed him into a much more uncompromising individual.

He was completely objective and unsentimental, a typical American, despite having an English mother. I could not build a close bond of friendship with Gerald; I was here because I was useful to him.

## CHAPTER 10. THE RUSSIAN MEETING

After their dinner in the hotel restaurant Russell Keldale and Olga spent some time on the dance floor of the hotel and then retired to bed. We heard the bed creaking but as there was no screaming or unusual noises we decided it was safe to leave our equipment on record. We went down onto the billiard room and enjoyed a couple of frames of snooker.

To be exact I enjoyed the game more than Gerald because he is a pool player by instinct and experience and his wham bam method of playing put him at a definite disadvantage when playing snooker. It was very good for my morale to be better than him at something.

The next morning after breakfast we heard them plan to go sightseeing in Birmingham. Being well acquainted with the area we followed them at a discreet distance down the hill into the Bull ring .This being the place where there is a rag market and hundreds of different market stalls sell different items. There has been a market here for well over 800 years.

Wife selling was quite common here in the early 18th Century.

The Bull ring provides space for religious and political agitators to literally get on a soap box and harangue the crowd.

A sandwich board man, with the notice hanging from his shoulders, REPENT or SUFFER THE ETERNAL DAMNATION OF HELL FIRE is always present and there are always a good number of street entertainer's fire eaters and men who specialise in getting out of chains. This place could provide cover for making contact many times over.

After a brief visit to the Digbeth Civic Hall and St Martins in the Bull Ring church we follow the couple back along New Street in the direction of the Town Hall and the War Memorial. We pass in front of the site of the pre Elizabethan King Edward School .This made me remember the words from our old school song 'for our pious founder King Edward the VI.`

The son of Henry the VIII he died in his early teens presumable before he had time to develop any bad habits.

Passing the Hall of memory we were quite surprised to see them cross over the road and disappear down Gas Street into the canal basin. This area consists of a maze of small canal side houses and ware houses.

" We have probable lost then "I said.

"Why?" asked Gerald "Because there are more miles of canals in Birmingham than there are in Venice?"

We hurried across the road and were just in time to see then board a narrow boat. "We cannot risk being spotted we had better find out if the boat returns to the same berth." Gerald said.

We gave the boat time to chug off at its steady 3 MPH and then went on to the small quay side office

“Excuse me Sir, who owns that boat?” Gerald asked his American accent betraying him immediately.

“A foreigner a quiet man keeps himself to himself, no trouble to anyone. A displaced person I think.

“Any other foreigners get on the boat?” Gerald asked`

" There were a couple, a big grim faced man straight backed , face like a bag of nails, the other one looked a bit like Hitler with a little black moustache.

“! Thank you Sir” said Gerald slipping a ten shilling note into the man’s hand

"Your friend Don’t arf speak queer you'd think boi now it woz time the rest of the wairld spowk loik us, wudden cha " said the genial boatman with a broad grin.

"Yow ave to mek allowances faw our colonial cussins, our kid” I replied.

Meanwhile on the boat unknown to us a small man carrying a copy of the times sat on the seat next to Russell Kildare

“You are an American? “asked the stranger.

"Yes Sir" said Keldale.

"This is your young lady Olga?”.

The eagle is a fine bird is it not?

The stranger fixed Russell with a hypnotic stare.

"Sure especially on a ten dollar coin.”

"They are very rare also, what have you got for me? " asked the second man turning round.

Russell saw with apprehension that it was Colonel Cupric. "

“I have some very interesting plans and documents for you. They are locked in the hotel safe at the moment. These plans and documents took a lot of work planning and risk they should be worth a lot of money."

“I will have to examine them to decide if they are worth anything. We will dine at your hotel tonight and then visit you at about 10 PM. Room 301 is it not. We will be staying at your hotel because we will be attending a Trade Show at Bingley Hall. We will not acknowledge each other if we happen to meet in the hotel, is that clearly understood? "

The thin lipped moustached man sat quietly and watched them

"OK Sir” said Russell.

The narrow boat cruised along the dirty oily water passing grimy warehouses and open spaces where houses had stood until they had been blasted into oblivion during the blitz.

Nature had started to reclaim her own and thistles weeds and rough grass had started to cover over some of the worst of the rubble. Derelict small boats and barges lined the canal banks many half submerged in the dank water. It was hard to imagine that this was once a thriving waterway the most important means of carrying goods for the most progressive and prosperous city during the industrial revolution.

We observed the boat return and Russell and Olga disembark. We then watched the other passengers disembark among them one man who we both recognised as Colonel Cupric from the photographs supplied to us by Colonel Dan Davies. We have seen them together; we had better report the contact to Headquarters.

We followed them back to the Victoria Hotel and while they were having lunch we telphoned through our report to Colonel Davies. The Colonel said that we have confirmed their suspicions about Keldale but they needed to know what information Keldale knows that could be of use to an important operative like Yuri Cupric. We were instructed to keep observing them and see if anything is handed over to the Russians.

After lunch we followed them to Warwickshire County Cricket Club, and enjoyed a pleasant afternoon's cricket. We heard Olga tell Russel that it was here in 1946 that Eric Hollies took all ten wickets in the first innings against Nott's without fielding aid, a record that will never be achieved again.

We were pleasantly surprised to find out that Olga was a cricket fan. The only other cricket fan that I knew was Corporal Keith Smart who bored the pants of me with his enthusiasm for the game, but his memory for details of matches was phenomenal.

Corporal Smart had taken over my job looking after the Wing Commanders charts and by all account was doing a good job and getting on very well with the Winco. They were both qualified accountants and therefore had a lot in common.

Corporal Smart was not quite so popular with the Adjutant because of a difference of opinion over some statistics that the Winco had been discussing with the Flt Lt.

Corporal Smart had glanced at the sheet and spotted an error immediately. This error was down to the Adjutant and he was none too pleased when this discrepancy was discovered without any real effort by a corporal. The bleating apology by the Adjutant for his error was not made any easier for the Adjutant, when the Winco said "Well the Corporal is qualified".

When this was told to me by Keith Smart I could not help but feel sorry for the Adjutant who had been outshone by a bright young man.

We followed Sgt Russell Keldale and Olga Newcastle back to the hotel and awaited developments.

We knew that Russell and Olga were dining at 8pm at the hotel so we settled ourselves comfortable at our table and kept a discreet observation on the couple in the dining room. We enjoyed the cream of tomato soup followed it by doing full justice to the roast sirloin of beef with Yorkshire pudding , roast and creamed potatoes, Brussels sprouts and buttered carrots.

We were enjoying the profiteroles with fresh cream, when a large stern faced man accompanied by a smaller man wearing a small black moustache entered the restaurant and was shown to a seat by the window.

It was Colonel Yuri Cupric of the KGB, with the little snake eyed man we had seen getting off the canal boat earlier. Things were beginning to hot up.

We had heard that Russel and Olga were planning to go dancing at the Locarno Ballroom in Hurst Street. The well-known Colin Hulme and his broadcasting band were appearing there, Olga was keen to get Russell there for an evening of dancing in pleasant surroundings.

Sonny Rose was at the West End ballroom, and Acker Bilk was also playing in Birmingham that week so there was plenty of choice for those who wished to enjoy the pleasure of ballroom dancing.

We wondered if the appearance of the two Russians would affect the plans of the two lovers for tonight. I did not realize just how much their appearance was to affect my life.

The Russians did not acknowledge the American or his girlfriend but were soon enjoying the fruits of the free enterprise system they were bent on destroying.

Russell and Olga finished their meal and I followed them back to their room. I picked up the head phones and listened in on their conversation.

"What are we to do? I heard Olga asking " Wait for them to contact us that was the instruction we were given." " I hope this is not going to spoil our nights dancing" " We have to wait and see" said Keldale "We are going dancing " said Olga " They do not own me "  "Shut up! This could be the most important night of your life that big guy is a very important man and I have to see him."

Even through the wall I could feel a distinct chilling in the atmosphere.

The door of our room opened and Gerald Beaufoy slipped quickly into the room." The Russians are on their way up in the elevator" he said.

We sat in our chairs in front of our recording apparatus and waited. We heard a sharp rap on the door next door and from our spy hole we observed the two Russians standing outside in the corridor. The door was opened and the two Russians disappeared from sight.

Gerald beckoned me and we settled down to listen to the conversations over the head phones

After a brief introduction Colonel Cupric said "What have you to show me to make my journey worthwhile?

I have a number of valuable items for you to see said Keldale importantly. "What do you think of this?" There was a few seconds silence.

"Where did you get this?" "From my base I photographed it from a plan on the station commander's wall"

"What is it?"

"It is a plan showing the location of all the Russian Missile sites in Europe."

"Do you think a copy of a plan of our own missile sites can be of any value to us?

The annoyed tones of the senior KGB officer were evident even through a brick wall. "What could it possible tell us that we do not already know?"

The note of dismay in Keldales voice was plain to hear as the truth of the Russian assessment sunk into the slow thinking Americans brain.

"Well what you think of these?" he asked there was a pause and a rustling of paper.

There was silence as the Russians examined whatever it was that Keldale had produced for inspection.

"This looks more promising we will need to evaluate it in detail. These lists are bulky and we may need to film them.

The list of men to be posted to witness atomic bomb experiments are interesting, but this list detailing the detachment of four RAF squadrons to the Sudan may be of more interest.

I will have to talk to my comrades in the diplomatic service." A note of warmth was creeping into the KGB Colonel voice. We will be in contact with you again very shortly.

## CHAPTER 11

## ESPIONAGE.

Talks about the revision of the 1936 Anglo- Egyptian Treaty had broken down in 1951. This involved the use of the Suez Canal Base which could only be guaranteed by an Anglo- Egyptian settlement. Washington had given unqualified support to Britain in the Anglo Egyptian negotiations.

Rioting mobs in Cairo and Alexandria in January 1952 had burnt British owned buildings and killed eight Europeans and Canadians.

The CIA had developed plans to support Arab leaders who would cooperate with Washington. Egypt had developed a new military training programme which planned to send 300 officers to the US for training. Among the officers that attended the six month intelligence course in Colorado was Ali Sabri the head of air force intelligence.

Ali Sabri was a secret supporter of Free Officers who had a very big part in the coup d'état in Egypt that overthrew King Farouk on the 16th of July 1952 and put General Mohammed Neguib as leader of the ruling junta in power. This junta included Colonel Nasser.

It was not lost on our politicians that the first assurances by the Free officers were given to the Americans.

King Farouk was the butt of every kind of joke by the British Public not only because he was so corrupt, but as it was later revealed that he possessed the world's greatest collection of pornography.

The fact that the Americans approved of the sale of arms to the new Egyptian government was the subject of very strong protests by the British who managed to postpone the shipments until the right of passage along the Suez Canal and the employment of technicians to ensure the proper operation of the canal were settled.

The sale of arms that could be used against us if the situation deteriorated was a very sensitive matter.

John Foster Dulles warned Mr Eden; 'This settlement has dragged on to a point where we cannot continue much longer without grave effect upon all our Arab relationships. If you felt that it was likely that there would soon be moves in the Suez matter which might produce agreement, we could still hold up briefly the delivery of the arms but our time is running out fast'

The Prime minister Mr Churchill threatened to go it alone in Egypt, and withdraw support for the US policy on Communist China.

It had only been last year that the State Department had asked the British to recognise King Farouk as King of the Sudan this we had refused to do.

The Foreign Office claimed the recognition Farouk would be a betrayal .

The Sudanese had been promised self-determination and self-government.

Mr Churchill was still a force to be reckoned with and with Anthony Eden and John Foster Dulles not seeing eye to eye the situation was very unpredictable.

The existence of a list detailing the movement of four British RAF Squadrons to the Sudan would be of as much interest to the CIA as the Russian KGB

Colonel Cupric and his assistant were excited to think that this unpromising recruit had stumbled onto what could be a means of causing a major rift in Anglo American relations.

It was clear that the Americans were backing the new regime in Egypt, but was there a plot by the Monarchist Churchill to place King Farouk back on the throne of Egypt and also install him as King of the Sudan, in order to retain control over the Suez Canal Zone?

Why were the British going to send this considerable force to the Sudan?

He would have to send this information to Moscow as soon as possible.

This information could not only bring about a split between the British and the Americans but could be used to drive the new government in Cairo to seek the aid of the Russians and deny the West her military bases in Egypt.

Colonel Cupric was well aware of the importance of the information he now possessed." I will take charge of these papers you will be well rewarded if these prove of any value" he said to Keldale. "I will be in contact with you again; I have to attend a trade mission for the next two days, so I will not be able to process this information until I return to Germany.

The next conversation we recorded on our tape machine was

"Can we go dancing now?"

"Sure Babe"

"Do not call me babe"

"OK Olga" replied Keldale.

Gerald and I decided that we had better telephone Colonel Dan Davies and report these developments. Gerald spoke briefly to his Commander and within the hour we were on our way back to Gloucester to report to him in person. The Sunbeam Talbot coupe covering the sixty mile journey at a record speed, and we arrived at the American Camp just before mid-night. We were immediately shown into the base Commander's office. To my surprise in addition to the Americans there was the Wing Commander Lawyer and the Flight Lieutenant Admin John Whitehead and also a grim faced Group Captain.

A tape machine was already in position on a table and after a few brief words of introduction the tapes we had made were played to a very attentive audience. After the tapes had been played Dan Davies stood up and thanked us for obtaining this information and suggested that we might like to leave them to their deliberations and go and have a coffee in the adjourning room. We were only to please to do this the presence of so much top brass was un-nerving.

The Group Captain addressed the meeting.

The apparent volatility posed by the overthrow of King Farouk and the emergence of a new regime under General Neguib in December 1952 has been recognised by her Majesties Government. The Foreign Secretary Mr Eden is well on course with a policy of accommodating Egyptian opinion by the withdrawal of British troops from the Canal Zone; in the face of the militant Arab nationalism, he believes the British presence there is insupportable.

The main outstanding difference with Egypt, being the policy towards neighbouring Sudan, this will be settled on the basis of Sudan achieving independence in 1954. Mr Churchill tried to sabotage this policy and at one stage proposed redeployment of two battalions of British troops and four RAF squadrons to Khartoum 'to restore order', following the pro-Egyptian demonstrations there.

According to Evelyn Shuckburg at the Middle East desk at the Foreign Office, Mr Churchill wanted to invent a reason for sending troops to Sudan in order to mask the 'disgrace' of withdrawing them from Egypt` there was brief talk of Mr Eden resigning . But the Foreign Secretary, with the backing of his colleagues, intends to get British forces redeployed to Cyprus, Libya, Jordan and the Persian Gulf instead. The Treaty still seems to be the only course, Mr Eden has told Churchill firmly.

Mr Churchill will be standing down soon in favour of Mr Eden. This information and the information on these tapes must remain confidential.

This information in the hands of the Russians would prove very embarrassing to HM Government. Every effort must be made to recover the details stolen from our Record Office of the so called preparations for the invasion of the Sudan.

The senior American officer then stood up and stated that he was authorised to say that the CIA were now in favour of encouraging and supporting Arab leaders who were friendly to Washington and that they now considered King Farouk a spent force.

They would co-operate in the recovery of the papers. They considered that the offer to sell the information to the communists by Sgt Keldale was treason and they would arrest him as soon as the papers were recovered.

We were told to go back into the room by the massive American Policeman who was guarding the door.

Colonel Dan Davies spoke to Gerald "Well Mr Beaufoy you and Mr Darby have done well to unmask these two traitors. We now have the problem of recovering the material they have obtained before Cupric leaves the country with it. If we arrest Keldale and Newcastle now, we will alarm Cupric and he may try to leave the country immediately. It is obvious he intends to leave the country at the end of the trade fair in that way he will cause no particular interest, and he will then be free to come here again at will.

What we want is to catch him with the documents, recover them before he can pass on any of them and then get him declared persona non gratia.

You are staying in the same hotel. Search his room, the recovery of these documents is top priority. We can deal with Keldale and his accomplice afterwards. Is that clear Gerald?" "Yes Sir" replied Gerald Beaufoy.

"Do you need any other help" "No Sir, Jack has been a great help and I can rely on him he knows the real estate on which we are working."

"We will arrange for someone to drive you back to the Hotel so that you can get some rest before you do what has to be done.

Are we in agreement gentlemen? "asked the Colonel turning to the other officers, who all nodded their assent. The Wing Commander lawyer and the Group Captain turned to me and to my surprise the Group Captain said "Well done Jack we are relying on you." The Wing Commander smiled his approval and said "Take care; this could be a dangerous affair."

"The flight Lieutenant Admin said "Well done Jack is there anything you need?"

"No thank you, everything is being taken care of thank you John" I said without blinking an eyelid.

The driver detailed drove us back to the hotel while I slept in the back of the car. Gerald did not seem to miss his sleep although I had a suspicion that he was taking a tablet to keep him going.

After our breakfast next morning we made our plan to recover the papers from Cupric. The next day we knew he would be at Bingley Hall attending the trade show as part of the Russian Delegation so we felt reasonable sure he would have left the papers in his hotel bedroom. We had to gain access to his suite after the chamber maids had done their morning cleaning. We knew that the cleaning was done as soon as the visitors left the hotel.

A 9AM breakfast saw Cupric and his party leave the hotel, we heard him inform the head waiter that they would not return until dinner that evening. That was good news for us, it gave us all day, if necessary, to search his room for the papers. By 11AM we were letting ourselves into the KGB officer's suite, with the pass key obtained from one of the chamber maids "How did you get the key Gerald?" "I gave the girl a pound and she was quite willing to be helpful.

We searched the room and found a large important looking black briefcase. It was on a shelf in the wardrobe that occupied part of the wall adjacent to the bed.

This seemed too easy to be true. The case was locked by a substantial lock. There was no was no way we could force the lock.

"Break it " said Gerald. I inserted the blade of my knife into the seam of the leather and cut the back out of the brief case .I shook the contents of the brief case onto the bed there were several files of papers with Russian titles on the front of the files.

We ignored these, but under them was a list headed TOP SECRET written in English. We opened the file in it were details of troops and RAF Squadrons that were to ready to be despatched at short notice to the Sudan.

There was also another list headed atomic bomb testing South Pacific. This was it. We sat on the bed we could not believe our luck in being able to retrieve these papers so easily.

Suddenly we heard a noise and we heard the door of the suite open. I froze in terror. Gerald motioned to me to stay silent.

Gerald took up his position behind the door and drew his automatic pistol from his shoulder holster. We waited as the footsteps crossed the room towards the bedroom.

The door opened and in stepped the dark-skinned man wearing a small dark moustache.

"Please sit down" said Gerald calmly pointing his pistol at the chest of the KGB man. "Comrade Torowski we are recovering some of our property I am angry that one of my country men would sell information to you .

Do not make any any quick movements but raise your hands in the air and keep them there.

Search him Jack approach him from the side and feel inside his coat to see if he is carrying a weapon."

I carried out a full body search "He is not armed " I reported to Gerald

"I wish to protest I demand....."

"Sit down Torowski"

"I have full diplomatic privileges. I demand to see the Soviet ambassador."

"You have abused the hospitality of the British government by engaging in espionage. Your ambassador will not be pleased that you have been caught. You will be sent back to Moscow in disgrace. We intend to take back our property, what you do is up to you comrade.

We will not harm you provided you do not interfere with us .

This is a comfortable posting for you, talk to Colonel Cupric before you decide on your next move." Gerald returned the pistol to its soft chamois shoulder holster.

We left the room with a subdued Russian sitting on a hard chair looking into space.

I knew at that moment that my life would not be quite the same again.

## CHAPTER 12

## MAKING THE BEST OF IT.

We returned to our room and Gerald telephoned through to the special number that we had been given to report any progress or to request any assistance.

We were told to avoid any further contact with the Russians and that a special unit would be contacting us to take charge of the papers , as evidence , to be used in connection with any action against Colonel Cupric and his partner know now to us as Captain Torowski.

We were however to keep observations on Russell Keldale and Olga Newcastle during the rest of their stay at the Victoria Hotel. Within an hour there were two tall smartly dressed men standing in the hall way outside our door. Looking through the spyhole we could see who they were before they spoke. They looked ex-service with short hair-cuts and military ties I asked "Who is it?" before we opened the door the reply came liked a burst of machine gun fire "Dan Davies has sent us, let us in quickly" On being admitted to the hotel room they produced Identity documents to the satisfaction of Gerald, who offered them a drink .

"Scotch?

"Thank you.

Where are the papers? "

Gerald produced the files and they were quickly placed in a leather suite case and locked in. " We do not give receipts but you can report the transfer of the documents to us by telephone to HQ now." This instruction was given with calm assurance of a man who was used to issuing orders and having them complied with without question.

Gerald picked up the phone and did as he was told.

The Special Unit man spoke clearly and distinctly with the carefully modulated tone associated with the officer class . There was something about his eyes that made me very wary of him. Then the realisation came to me that he had the same look that I had seen in the eyes of Gerald Beaufoy. They finished their drinks and left the apartment.

" Glad to see those two go ?" said Gerald.

I nodded my agreement.

"I think we deserve to treat ourselves to another visit to the cabaret Club to-night to celebrate our success" said Gerald .

"A good idea I do not suppose we will have many more nights here then it will be back to camp.

"After this I am sure they will offer you something , most likely a good promotion . I expect to get promotion to captain for my part in this."

I looked at Gerald quickly. " So you are an officer already "I said . "Sure I was going to tell you I am a lieutenant in the US intelligence Corps , I have been working undercover as a sergeant in order to keep my eye on Sergeant Keldale.

Sorry to have kept this from you but it was really on a need to know basis, and for the purpose of this operation it was better for you to think that I was a sergeant.

You remember Samantha from the Cabaret Club I will give her a ring and we will see if she can fix you up with a friend from the Repertory company and we will go out for dinner. O K."

"Yes. It might be a long time before I get another chance like this"

After a good four course meal in a small discreet restaurant close to the Birmingham Rep. we caught a taxi to Edgbaston .The actress friend of Samantha turned out to be a tall blonde by the name of Simone She was one of those self-confident extroverts with a pretty face and the soft valley of her cleavage eliminated any thought of criticism of the choice of my blind date.

Simone and I had parted company with Gerald and Samantha, after the meal.

An hour later we were lying on a large white double bed with my hand fondling an ample breast that was clearly available .

“What do you do?” I asked.

"Anything that you would want "was her reply.

Simone smiled and kissed me with genuine enthusiasm.

Afterwards as we sat talking in the bed supported up by ample feather pillows Simone turned leaning on one elbow her breasts swinging towards my face. She saw the look of lust and appreciation and smiled.

"I bet Gerald and Samantha have been doing the same thing" I said remembering my ally.

The smile went from Simone's face . "You wouldn't want what she does. She does not do straight sex. She only does SM. "

"What is SM? " I asked.  She smiled again "You are an innocent " she said.

The look of hurt must have shown because after a pregnant pause Simone said "Would you like to be beaten with a cane on your bottom until it is red and bleeding? "

The look of shock and unbelief must have shown because she laughed and said "I don't fancy it either.

Your mate has a different personality to you. Did you notice how flat chested Samantha is?

No ! Well I think you have had enough shocks for one day.

Come here! " Her mouth was soft and I enjoyed the ecstasy of the moment, again.  "You can stay the night if you want to?"  I did.

The next morning we sat and had coffee and I became aware the girl was not breathtakingly beautiful but that her big blue eyes looked clearly and unemotionally at me over the table . Simone had the well-toned physique of a professional dancer and her generous chest was enclosed in a pink silk top.

"Shall I ring for a taxi for you? I have to go to rehearsals later "she said .

"Yes Please.  Thank you."

I returned to earth. I took a note of her telephone number, Simone said  "I will be pleased to see you again, but make sure you ring me first."

I never did ring her or see her again.

The taxi dropped me at the Victoria hotel and I made my way into the hotel past the porter who said "Good morning Sir" with an embarrassingly knowing smile. I made my way to the suite that I shared with Gerald.

Two large uniformed policemen stood guard at the door of the next suite.

The door of the suite occupied by Olga and Russell Keldale opened and a body covered in a blanket was carried out.

## CHAPTER 13 .

## TOP SECRET REVEALED

"Corporal Stanley Bunker you are charged that contrary to Queens Regulations and Air Force Discipline ; You did wilfully misuse-use Air force property in that you did use an Air Ministry stamp to stamp the words TOP SECRET on the abdomen of a member of the Women's Royal Air Force. Namely senior aircraftswoman Thelma Lovit.

How do you plead?"

"Not guilty Sir"

Flight Lieutenant Whitehead entered the plea of not guilty on the charge sheet form 252."

What have you to say in answer to the charge?"

"Sir I was of duty waiting to meet SACW Lovit' at the office intending to take her out to the camp cinema after she came off duty. SACW Lovit was delayed at work doing some urgent typing for you Sir. Unfortunately by the time she finished this work we had missed the bus back to the camp. We were compelled to stay here for an hour waiting for the next transport back to camp. We were courting Sir, so we decided to find somewhere quiet to have a ' snog' Sir."

"Had it just been a quiet 'snog as you term it Corporal you would not be up on this charge.

" Why did you allow it escalate into this disgraceful escapade?

show the accused the photograph."

The warrant officer in charge of the detail produced a photograph and showed it to Corporal Bunker. The photograph showed the naked lower half of an obvious female body with the words TOP SECRET stamped as near as was possible to the lowest portion of her torso.

Stanley Bunker's mind could be seen to be working overtime as he mentally fought whether to brazen this out and deny any connection with the photograph, or to admit his guilt in taking the photograph and hope to get away with a smaller punishment.

"Well Corporal I am waiting for your explanation" said the Flt. Lt Admin who was sitting in judgement in his capacity as a subordinate commander.

"Well Sir I thought it was a bit of a joke at the time Sir."

"So you admit to the stamping now, do you?"

"Yes Sir"

"How did you come to obtain possession of this important stamp?

"The stamp was in a little stand on top of SACW Lovit's desk Sir"

"You had the audacity to use the Admin Office for your amorous adventures Corporal"

"Well it was the quietest place once the other airwoman had left Sir"

"What other airwoman?"

"LACW Olga Newcastle Sir."

"You saw LACW Newcastle that evening?"

"Yes Sir she travelled back to camp with us on the later bus."

"You could swear to that"

"Yes Sir"

"This is a most serious offence you have committed Corporal that could result in you being demoted and losing your stripes but on the other hand I could enter a reprimand on your service documents . Because of the seriousness of the charge I am going adjoin the case for consideration for five days.

March them out Mr Frazer"

"Accused and escort, right turn, quick march."

Corporal Stanley Bunker and his escort of peer's are marched out.

Corporal Bunker is left to sweat about retaining his stripes while more serious matters are considered.

What Flt Lt. Whitehead did not know was Corporal Bunker had been doing a nice steady trade in the camp selling copies of this photograph to curious national servicemen .

Bunker had built quite a reputation in selling saucy photographs, this one out selling his previous best photograph of a young lady standing on a glass topped table while wearing only a big smile.

Flight Lieutenant Whitehead's next job is to ascertain where Olga Newcastle was, and what she was doing between finishing work and catching the later bus back to camp. Olga would have finished her work and be ready to leave at the normal time. The dour Olga was a good typist despite lacking in charm, and it had never been necessary for her to be detained to work late to finish her tasks for the day. So why did she not catch the transport at the normal time?

The authority to remain in the section and work late could only be given by the officer in charge and he certainly had not given LACW Newcastle permission to work late.

Olga Newcastle was due back from leave in two days' time , but he felt that he had better report his findings to the Wing Commander, straight away.

This piece of evidence was placed before the Winco Admin who recognised that this would have given her the time and the opportunity to obtain access to the South Pacific postings lists, and the list of the RAF squadrons that were detailed for despatch at short notice to the Sudan.

"Good work spotting that Whitehead , I will pass the information on along the line . This should enable the SIB to complete their investigations and could well be conclusive in proving that LACW Newcastle was the one who betrayed us. The quicker this matter is cleared up the better. The Air Ministry and the Foreign Office have got involved. A leakage of this kind is an embarrassment for the government. The speedy solving of this problem will be appreciated at the highest level ,and any contribution we make will be recognised. Your name will appear in my report John"

"Thank you Sir" replied the delighted Administrative Officer.

"I think you could let that Corporal Bunker off with a severe reprimand this time. At any proceedings against Newcastle he may be called to give evidence. The evidence of a man reduced to the ranks would not have the same weight as that of an NCO. Agreed?"

"Yes Sir. That is what I thought" replied John Whitehead dutifully

"Corporal Bunker admitted taking the photographs then. Quite an artist with the camera I see. The subject matter is your other typist. A pleasant girl. I must have a word with her commanding officer. I have never detected any malice in her and she performed well at the camp concert last year."

Flight Lieutenant Whitehead was not sure but he thought he detected a gleam in the Wing Commanders eye. He did remember that as a member of the dance troupe Thelma had been applauded and encored for her high kicking routine, during the last concert. The Winco recommending her for an extra 48 hour pass for her work in the show.

Ten minutes later the camp commander was on the phone to the wing commander. "I have been informed that LACW Olga Newcastle has been arrested by the special investigations branch in Birmingham. It is unlikely she will return to this unit. I will keep you informed."

The flight lieutenant admin had already started on his procedures to replace Olga Newcastle with considerable enthusiasm. This was confirmation of his judgement that he had seen the last of her.

He was reconciled that he would be keeping corporal Smart to keep the establishment charts going. The corporal was an asset to any office and showed the respect that was due from a junior non-commissioned officer to a man holding the Queens Commission.

While Corporal Jack Darby had shown the same respect, he was not sure that exposure to the more lax American discipline had not affected that young man .After all he had called him 'John' with an almost casual air only a week ago.

## CHAPTER FOURTEEN

## BACK TO EARTH

I stopped dead in my tracks. The two uniformed policemen looked menacingly at me.

"What do you want" demanded the smaller of them."

" I am staying here" I replied "What has happened"

"None of your business" replied the surly one eyeing me a great deal of suspicion.

The smart special investigations branch officer followed the two men carrying the body out of the room.

"All correct Sir" reported the uniformed constable, saluting smartly across the body.

"This young man has been assisting us in our surveillance of this suite, it is in order for him to pass."

"Very good Sir" said the constable.

I wondered who they were carrying out, then Gerald Beaufoy appeared.

"I guess you are entitled to see who this is."

Gerald drew the covering back from the face of the corpse.

The white waxen face of Russell Keldale looked up at me . His face was distorted and bitter looking. The sightless eyes were devoid of any expression. There was blood by his ear and on his neck .

This was a sudden and violent death even to my untrained eye.

I turned to one side feeling slightly sick at the sight. I entered the suite and saw to my surprise that there were a number of men searching the room.

" Where is Olga Newcastle?" I enquired.

"She has been arrested. Your job here is now done You are to report back to Flight Lieutenant Whitehead."

This cold matter of fact statement was given by the SIB man, the smart suite and cultured accent could not disguise the deadly efficiency of his manner. The steel grey eyes deep set in a strong face clearly said no more questions.

I was pleased to get back into my bedroom and pack my belongings ready for the return to rural Gloucestershire.

Gerald Beaufoy came into the room and started to do his packing in his usual methodical way, When he took of his jacket to change for the journey I noticed that the soft leather holster containing the pistol were missing .

I thought it prudent not to ask any questions.

Reporting to the Administrative Office the next day Corporal Keith Smart who was sitting in the chair that I had occupied for over twelve months gleefully informed me that I was no longer on the strength of the Admin. Office and that he was the permanent incumbent of that seat until he completes his engagement.

Thelma greeted me with a smile and a wink

Somebody had put in a good word for her and she had got off with a reprimand from a WRAF officer and a few extra domestic duties.

There was a pretty girl sitting in the seat that Olga had occupied.

A young pilot officer poked his head round the door.

"Flight Lieutenant Whitehead will see you now Corporal."

"Good morning Sir" I said to John Whitehead . It had only been a few short weeks since I stood in that office, but it was a very much more confident and experienced 20 year old that stood in front of the Flt Lt Admin. that morning.

I have been instructed to remind you that the duties that you have just completed are subject to the Official Secrets Act, in the same manner as any other information you may have acquired.

Do you understand that Corporal?"

The look of weariness following the traumatic last 48 hours must have shown on my face because John Whitehead then said "Sit down Corporal I understand that Sgt Keldale and LACW Newcastle have been arrested."

The scene in that hotel bedroom flashed through my mind, the sight of Keldale on that stretcher with his waxen face and his dim wide open pale blue eyes was clearly etched in my mind. The single bullet hole in the chest.

My first experience of sudden violent death.

My new maturity of thought and instinct made me give the discreetly correct answer that was required

"Yes Sir " I replied.

"You are to attend a de- briefing, you will then be given 14 days leave after that you are to be posted. I am sorry to lose you Corporal, the powers to be are pleased with your work. There will be an offer of promotion coming your way"

The young pilot officer nodded his approval.

My absence from normal austere service life and a taste of the comparatively luxurious life of the last few weeks had raised my expectations of and appreciation's of the good things in life.

The prospect of returning to a small room at the end of a billet full of snoring deadly farters did not appeal to me one little bit."

At the debriefing held at the American Air base I learnt from Colonel Dan Davies that Sgt Russel Keldale had lost his life while serving his country, and would be receiving a posthumous award for assisting in the recovery of secrets for an ally, from communist agents.

Lieutenant Beaufoy was to be promoted to Captain and to receive another medal. The Wing Commander Lawyer told me directly "We are pleased with the way you have conducted yourself in this matter. The recovery of the information was a first class job. The matter will now be dealt with at a very highest level. You must say nothing to anybody about these matters, As far as you are concerned these events did not take place.

"For several long moments his eyes searched my face.

"Agreed?" I felt firmer, stronger and wiser in the presence of this senior officer. "Yes Sir" I replied.

"Sensible man enjoy your leave. We reward loyalty. You will be promoted on your return."

Olga Newcastle was charged and appeared at her trial pleading through her defending officer that she acted under the coercion of her lover.

Statements had been obtained from the American authorities that Sgt Russell Keldale had a wife living in Germany during the period that he had been courting Olga. There was no way that he would be able to marry Olga as he had promised. This fact was used to great effect by the defending officer who was able to portray Olga as a badly used woman

Due to the fact of her admitting the offences with which she was charged she received the minimum sentence that the court could impose. This meant that because of the time she had spent in open arrest while waiting for her case to be heard she was freed one week after the trial was finished.

During the evidence it emerged that after she had copied the records of the postings Olga had seen a light on in the Admin Office, and had gone to the office next door and seen Corporal Stanley Bunker taking photographs of a half-naked Thelma, who was a very willing accomplice in the making of the photographic record of their love making.

In her spite she had reported the fact to her WRAF officer.

Olga was not to know that her vindictive action would lead to her own downfall.

In the event the Corporal Stanley Bunker did not lose his stripes and it was understood that he did very well out of his amorous escapade.

Thelma found herself more popular than ever.

A few months later Colonel Yuri Cupric and his assistant Captain Stokowski were expelled from Britain and disappeared into the vastness of the Soviet Empire.

Towards the end of 1953 the Egyptian government announced the sale of the royal treasures. The sale would include everything, from priceless objects d'art to rubbishy bric-a brac which the exiled king had stored in every palace. Neguib's government approached Sotheby's in London to catalogue the collection and organise the auction.

It took Sotheby's experts more than three months to sift and arrange the hoard. They had to sell the largest stamp collection in the world, some eight thousand five hundred coins and medals in gold, and one hundred and sixty -four in platinum, and one thousand two hundred and sixty-one works of art in gold and silver which included exquisite boxes, clocks and ornaments by the great Russian jeweller and goldsmith Carl Faberge.

Some of the experts recoiled with horror when they observed how the army guards were treating the collections. With a Faberge egg which realised six thousand four hundred pounds in the sale they were playing football!

The mechanism of several rare Swiss snuff-boxes which showed lovers in various positions had almost been exhausted by the soldiers, who had given them more to do in three months than they ever had in the King's possession.

Before the bidding started, an army spokesman announced that any one bidding over five thousand pounds during the auction would have a free tour of the pornographic museum.

Those who got the biggest kick out of the erotica were three American spinsters who ran with horror to their ambassador to protest at such filth. Few other people were shocked by the exhibits .The show case of pornographic books, opened at the most titillating pages, had as there centre piece, a picture of Lady Chatterley's Lover. The game keeper was one of the Kings favourite literary characters, or so they said.

Conclusion Mr Churchill told the Cabinet, on the 7th July 1954. " In spite of his earlier doubts he was now satisfied that the withdrawal of British troops from, Egypt could be fully justified on military grounds . Our requirements in the Canal zone had been radically changed by the admission of Turkey to the North Atlantic Treaty Organisation and the extension of a defensive Middle Eastern front as far east as Pakistan. Furthermore, the advent of thermonuclear weapons had greatly increased the vulnerability of a concentrated base area and it would not be right to retain in Egypt 80, 000 troops who could be better placed elsewhere."

On the seventeenth of March 1965 ex-king Farouk was dining with his latest girlfriend, Anna Maria Gatti, a hairdresser, at one hour before midnight he had eaten a dozen oysters, lobster Thermidor, a double portion of roast lamb with fried potatoes and French beans; he refused the crepes because they had put alcohol in then, but he took a huge helping of trifle, which he washed down with his second bottle of Evian Water.

He lit his cigar and then he died.

Oxygen and heart stimulants failed to resuscitate him, he never regained consciousness.

At forty -five years of age ex-king Farouk lay dead in a Rome morgue.

On the 27th of March he was flown by Comet to be buried in secret in Cairo with his feet pointing towards Mecca.

END

**BY THE SAME AUTHOR.**

**HENRY BURTON THE LIFE OF A VICTORIAN POLICEMAN**

**NEARLY 60 YEARS SERVICE IN LONDON, BIRMINGHAM, DUDLEY, & WORCESTSHIRE.**

24565393R00066

Printed in Poland
by Amazon Fulfillment
Poland Sp. z o.o., Wrocław